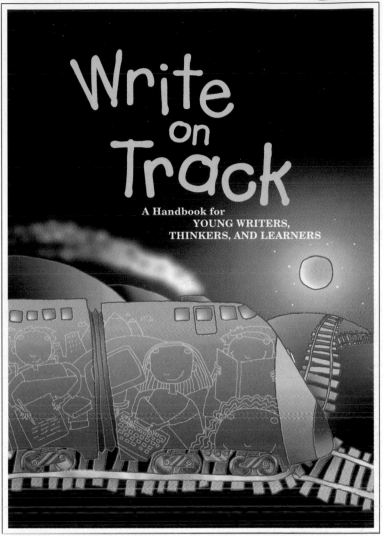

Write on Track

A Handbook for
YOUNG WRITERS,
THINKERS, AND LEARNERS

Authors
Dave Kemper, Ruth Nathan, Patrick Sebranek

Illustrator
Chris Krenzke

WRITE SOURCE®
GREAT SOURCE EDUCATION GROUP
a Houghton Mifflin Company
Wilmington, Massachusetts

Acknowledgements

We're grateful to many people who helped bring *Write on Track* to life. First, we must thank all the students from across the country who contributed their writing models and ideas.

Also, thanks to the writers, editors, and teachers who helped make this book a reality.

Susan Ohanian	Candyce Norvell
Dennis Andersen	Stephen Krensky
Rebecca Davison	Myra Zarnowski
Charles Temple	Allan Wolf

In addition, we want to thank our Write Source team for all their help: Heather and Laura Bachman, Colleen Belmont, Carol Elsholz, Tom Gilding, Beverly Jessen, Lois Krenzke, Sherry Schenning-Gordon, Julie Sebranek, Sandy Wagner, and Dawn Weis.

Printed in the United States of America

International Standard Book Number: 0-669-40880-8 (hardcover)
        9 10 -RRDC- 02 01 00 99

International Standard Book Number: 0-669-40881-6 (softcover)
        11 12 -RRDC- 02 01 00

Get on the Right Track!

The *Write on Track* handbook is divided into five parts:

1 **The Process of Writing** ● This part will help you learn all about writing, from selecting a subject to checking a final draft.

2 **The Forms of Writing** ● Would you like to start a journal, write a poem, or create a time-travel fantasy? Then this section is for you!

3 **The Tools of Learning** ● Reading, vocabulary, speaking, and test taking are all important skills. This part covers them all.

4 **The Proofreader's Guide** ● Have a question about punctuation? Spelling? Capitalization? You'll find help here.

5 **The Student Almanac** ● Full-color maps, a historical time line, math tables—*Write on Track* is truly an all-school handbook!

Table of Contents

The **PROCESS** of Writing

The FORMS of Writing

The TOOLS of Learning

The Proofreader's GUIDE

The Student ALMANAC

Why Write?

A Note from the Editors

Many things are good for you, including fresh air and green vegetables. Writing is good for you, too. The students listed here will tell you why:

- Writing keeps my past in my memory.

  —Joseph Clayton Leonard

- Writing introduces me to the outside world.

  —Molly Dyer

- I like to write because I can use my imagination.

  —Rachel Dietrich

- I build a lot of confidence when I write.

  —Chelsea King

- I like to write because it helps me express my feelings, and it's fun.

  —Lauren Evans

Writing for Good Reasons

Why write? These students have offered some very good reasons. Writing helps them remember and learn. It helps them make up stories and share their feelings. And writing is fun to do, which really makes it a good thing!

Write on Track can help you enjoy writing, too. It is loaded with ideas and examples for all of the writing you will do. It also has a special section called "The Proofreader's Guide" that will help you put capital letters and periods in the right places. Always have your copy of the handbook next to you when you write.

A Big, Little Book

Guess what? *Write on Track* will also help you tell stories, become a better speller, study for tests, learn about history, and much more. In other words, it will help you stay on track with all of your schoolwork. Not bad for one little book.

Have fun using *Write on Track*. And good luck with your writing and learning. **Remember:** Something can be good for you (like writing) and still be a lot of fun!

1 The Process of Writing

Getting Started

All About Writing

"There's nothing I like better than writing!"

Those are the words of Emily Martin, a student like you. Here are some more things Emily said.

"Making up a story is like making a movie, and I get to decide exactly how it's done. I also like to write letters, thank-you notes, and happy-birthday notes. I like to write about my life and what happens."

Writing is many different things.

Emily's words say a lot about writing. They tell us that writing can be fun. They also tell us that writing is a way to talk to others, and a way to learn about ourselves. No wonder Emily likes writing!

What else do you need to know about writing? Well, read on to find out. *Write on Track* tells you all about writing.

The Writing Process in Action

Writers like Emily use the **writing process**. The steps in the writing process are listed on the next two pages. You should follow these steps when you write your own stories, reports, and other things. The writing process will help you do your best work—just like it helps Emily and other writers!

The Writing Process

* **Select** a subject.
* **Collect** details about your subject.
* **Decide** what you want to say about it.

Prewriting
Planning Your Writing

Writing the First Draft

* **Get** all of your ideas on paper.
* **Don't** worry about making mistakes.

Revising
Improving Your Writing

* **Read** and review your first draft.
* **Share** your draft with another person.
* **Make** changes to improve your writing.

Editing and Proofing

* **Make** sure that your sentences and words make sense.
* **Check** your spelling, capital letters, and punctuation.
* **Write** a neat final copy of your work.
* **Check** one last time for errors.

Publishing

* **Share** your writing.
* **Submit** it to a class book or newspaper.
* (See pages 30-33 for other ideas.)

One Writer's

Process

Peter Jones had to write about an event he will always remember. Here's how he used the writing process to complete his work.

1 Prewriting: Planning the Writing

Selecting a Subject ● Peter thought of two great story ideas. He could write about the time he broke his arm, or the time he raced in the pinewood derby. He decided to write about the derby because he had so much fun, and he remembered a lot about it.

Collecting Details ● Next, Peter started listing details about this event.

my car ran great,
winning one race,
getting a trofe,
giving high fives,
my friends winning,
people taking pictures...

After listing these details, Peter was ready to write his first draft. (You can read it on the next page.)

Writing the First Draft

2

   In his first draft, Peter put all of his ideas on paper. He didn't worry about making mistakes.

A Day at the Pinewood Derby

   I was in the pinewood derby and it was neat and I won.

   I didn't win the first time. In the pinewood derby, they have a lot of different races. Every car gets to race more than once. In the second race, my car took off like a shot! And before I could say awesome, I won!

   I got a trofe. Everybody congragelated me. I gave a lot high fives.

   My friends Marcy and Eric won races, too. Cory won a trofe for best appearance. A guy took a picture of all four of us. I was kneeling down in front

   When I got home my mom took another picture. I was holding my car in one hand and my trofe in the other one. Mom said the trofe was heavy. The picture was blury. I said it was okay. Then I felt really tired, so I went to bed.

3 Revising: Improving the Writing

Peter read his first draft and had one of his parents read it, too. Then he changed different parts. Here's how he changed the first two paragraphs.

changed idea ┈┈┈► It was one of the best

I was in the pinewood derby, ~~and it was neat and~~

days of my life.

~~I won.~~ ┈┈ **moved idea**

(I didn't win the first time.) In the pinewood derby,

they have a lot of different races. Every car gets to

race more than once. In the second race, my car took

off like a shot! And before I could say awesome,

I won! I was so surprised. ◄┈┈┈┈ **added idea**

4 Editing and Proofreading

Next, Peter made sure that all his sentences and words made sense. Then he checked for spelling and punctuation errors. (He also checked for errors after he wrote his final copy.) Here's how he edited the fourth paragraph.

My friends Marcy and Eric won races, too.

trophy

Cory won a ~~trophe~~ for best appearance. A ~~guy~~ photographer

took a picture of all four of us. I was kneeling down

in front

Publishing

5

Peter shared his story with his classmates. He also included his story in a class book and added pictures to make it more interesting.

A Day at the Pinewood Derby

I was in the pinewood derby. It was one of the best days of my life.

In the pinewood derby, they have a lot of different races. Every car gets to race more than once. I didn't win the first time. In the second race, my car took off like a shot! And before I could say awesome, I won! I was so surprised.

I got a trophy. Everybody congratulated me. I gave a lot of high fives.

My friends Marcy and Eric won races, too. Cory won a trophy for best appearance. A photographer took a picture of all four of us. I was kneeling down in front.

When I got home, my mom took another picture. I was holding my car in one hand and my trophy in the other one. The picture was blurry, but I said it was okay. Then I felt really tired, so I went to bed. What a day!

> I like writing with a computer because you can write faster and change things easier.
>
> —Travis De Wolf

Writing with a Computer

A long, long time ago, writers used a stylus (*say* `sti-ləs) to carve letters in clay tablets. Later on, they used quill pens to write on parchment (an animal skin). Not too long ago, they all used typewriters. The most popular tool for writing today is the **personal computer**.

Getting Started

This chapter will introduce you to writing with a computer. Once you get started, you will see why the computer has become a writer's best friend!

Getting to Know PC

I'm a personal computer—**PC** for short. From my monitor to my mouse, I am your personal writing friend. It's important that you know my basic parts.

1 My brain is located in the **computer** part. This is where I store information.

2 My **monitor** is where you see your work.

3 You enter your writing on my **keyboard.**

4 My **mouse** doesn't squeak. But it does help you move around on the monitor.

5 This is a **disk.** You put it in the computer to save your writing.

6 You can print a neat copy of your writing on the **printer**.

Using a Computer

Knowing about the basic parts of a computer is important. But that's not the whole story. You really need to understand a few more things.

 Remember that a computer can't think or write for you. You still have to come up with the words and ideas.

 Learn how to keyboard. That's how you enter your ideas into the computer. (Starting on the next page, you can learn about the keyboard.)

 Practice using the *word-processing program* in your computer. (This program makes your computer work as a writing machine.) To practice, enter one of your paragraphs or stories. Then try adding or changing words, checking your spelling, saving your work, and printing.

 Decide on the best way to use a computer. Many students do their planning and first drafts on paper. Then they enter their writing on the computer to make changes.

Using a computer is not always easy. Ask for help or check the computer manual when you get stuck.

Working with a Keyboard

What is a keyboard?

The **keyboard** links you to the computer. You use a pencil to write on paper; you use a keyboard to write on a computer. A keyboard is pictured on the next page.

What do all of the keys mean?

Most of the keys are easy to figure out. Here are four of them you may not know about:

* Use the *tab key* to indent the first line of a paragraph.
* Use the *shift key* to make capital letters and some punctuation marks.
* Use the *space bar* to make a space between your words.
* Use the *delete key* to erase a mistake.

How do you use the keyboard?

At first, you'll *hunt* for the right key and *peck* at it with a finger. That's okay, but it's not very fast.

Turn the page, and you'll see two strange-looking hands. When you learn how to keyboard, all of your fingers will be busy hitting the keys marked on each finger in the picture.

TIP: You can practice keyboarding right in your handbook! To get started, place your fingers on the "home row" on the keyboard. (The home row is the dark row of keys.)

Computer Keyboard

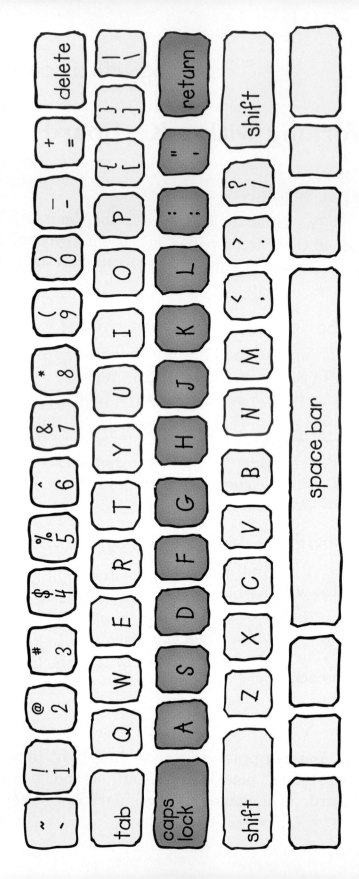

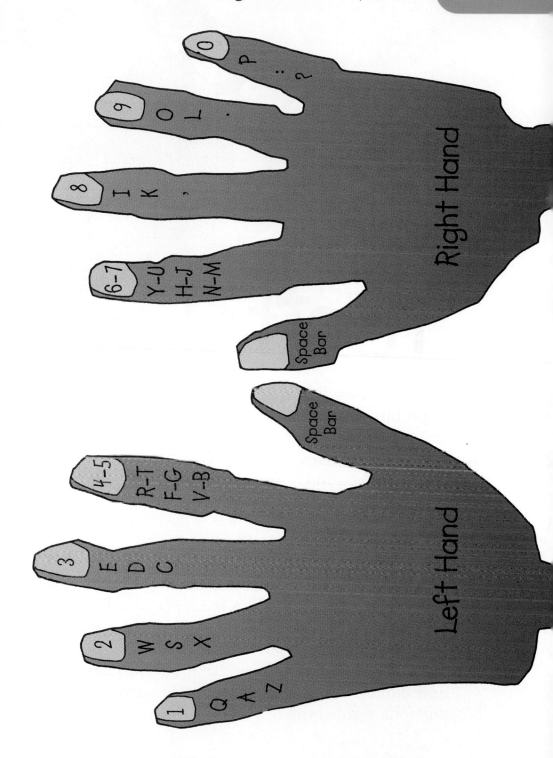

Right Hand

Left Hand

Space Bar

Space Bar

Planning
Portfolios

Jason Laws is a student who thinks that writing is very special. He says, "Writing is a gift that you won't forget." We think that writing is special, too. Another student named Jamey Fleming says, "It's fun to look back and see what you did." We agree.

A Special Place

This chapter is about planning portfolios (*say* pōrt-`fō-lē-ōs). A portfolio is a special collection of your writing. You'll learn about planning a **personal portfolio** (just for you) and a **classroom portfolio** (for school). If you like writing as much as Jason and Jamey do, then you'll want to start your own portfolio right away.

Making a Personal Portfolio

A **personal portfolio** is for you. You can set it up in a three-ring binder, in pocket folders, or in some other way. In one part, you could save all of your stories. In another part, you could save your poems, and so on.

You could also divide it into these four parts:

New Ideas

In one part, collect ideas for new writing projects. Keep lists of surprising sights, interesting thoughts, new sayings, and so on.

Writing in the Works

In another part, store your present projects. Maybe you're working on a nature poem or a true story.

Secret Writing

In a third part, keep copies of secret poems and notes.

Writing to Share

In a fourth part, save your completed work. The stories and poems in this part are ready to share.

Making a Classroom Portfolio

If you do a lot of writing in your class, your teacher may ask you to make a **classroom portfolio**.

Why is a classroom portfolio important?

A classroom portfolio helps you and your teacher think about your writing. It makes the writing process much more real and important to you.

What should you put into your portfolio?

Most of the time, a classroom portfolio will include examples of your best writing. It may also include evaluation or think sheets that ask questions about your writing.

Which pieces do you like best?

What writing skills have you learned?

What skills do you need to work on?

What is the most important thing to remember about your portfolio?

A classroom portfolio is the story of your own writing experiences. Take pride in it!

Writing is like a present to me. Our class writes every day.

—Carl Thomason

Planning Tips

When you plan a classroom portfolio, follow these tips:

Follow your teacher's directions.

* **Know what your portfolio should look like.**
  Your teacher may give you a folder to use or ask you to design your own.
* **Know what to include.**
  Know how many pieces of writing you should include. Also find out what think sheets you should complete.

Be organized.

* **Save all of your writing work.**
  Your teacher may ask you to include all of the notes and drafts for some of your writing.

Keep up.

* **Do each writing assignment on time.**
  Also complete all other parts of your portfolio when they are assigned.
* **Do your best work from start to finish.**
  Keep everything neat and organized.

Ask for help when you have a question about your portfolio, or about a writing assignment. It's important that you stay on track with all of your work.

Publishing
Your Writing

Publishing is the last step in the writing process. It means sharing one of your poems, stories, plays, or letters. Amy L. George is a student writer who loves this step in the process:

• The writing process is like a birthday party. When the party is over, I share my favorite presents, my stories.

Making Contact

Reading a story to your classmates is one way to publish; so is posting a poem on a class bulletin board. There are many other exciting ways to publish your best writing. You can learn about some of them on the next three pages.

Five Cool Publishing Ideas

Mail It!

* Mail a family story or a special poem to a relative.
* Share an adventure story with a friend who has just moved.
* Write a fan letter to someone you admire.
* Write a letter to a company or a public office asking for information.

Act It Out!

- Act out one of your plays with the help of your classmates.
- Perform one of your stories or poems. (See pages 240-245 for guidelines for performing a poem.)
- Tell one of your stories on videotape so faraway friends and relatives can enjoy it.
- Read one of your best pieces of writing to a parent/teacher group.

Print It!

- Put together a book of your own stories or poems. Or put together a class book. (See the next page for help.)
- Print a class newspaper.
- Make copies of book reviews for the school library.
- Make a picture book for younger students.
- Fax a poem to a family member at work.

Send It Out!

The magazines listed below publish student stories, poems, and letters. But they only print a few! Send your work to the magazine editor. Always include a self-addressed stamped envelope. (Ask your teacher for help.)

Highlights for Children
Children's Mail
803 Church Street
Honesdale, PA 18431

Young Voices
PO Box 2321
Olympia, WA 98507

Skipping Stones
PO Box 3939
Eugene, OR 97403

Stone Soup
PO Box 83
Santa Cruz, CA 95063

Bind It!

Make your own book by following these steps:

1. Put together your writing. Include a title page.

2. Staple or sew the pages together.

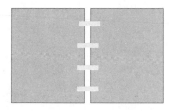

3. Cut two pieces of cardboard a little larger than the page size. Tape them together.

4. Place the cardboard on contact paper. Turn the edges of this material over the cardboard.

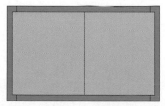

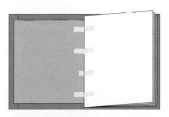

5. Glue a piece of paper to the inside of the cover.

6. Tape the pages into the cover.

Prewriting and Drafting Guide

Building a File of Writing Ideas

Sometimes, the hardest part of writing is finding a subject to write about. The job is a lot easier if you **build a file of writing ideas**. To get started, you have to think and act like a writer. That means you must always be on the lookout for interesting topics. Student writer Brett Mitchell knows all about finding ideas:

> You can do anything you want. When you see or hear something good, write it down. Just write it down!

Get a Notebook!

Keep all of your ideas in a notebook, where they'll be ready for your next writing assignment. This chapter tells you some fun ways to build a file of writing ideas.

Look, Listen, and Learn

1 **Keep your eyes open.** Sometimes a subject finds you! You might look up and see a hawk. You wonder about it. Where does it live? What does it eat? Write down this subject in your notebook, along with a few questions.

2 **Draw a life map.** Put in important events in your life. Start with the day you were born. Then check your map when you need a writing idea.

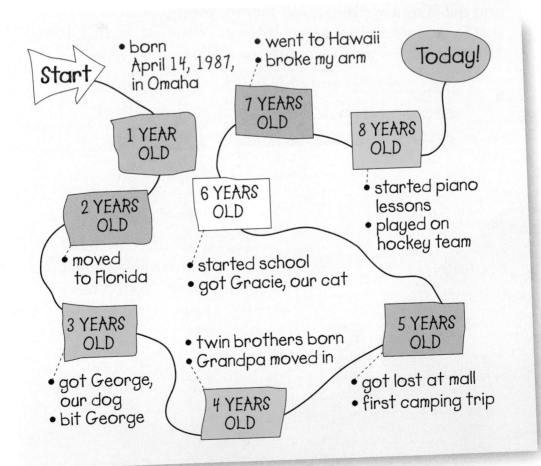

Make a list of your bests, worsts, and favorites. Here are a few ideas to get you started:

BESTS: My best days
              My best friends
              The things I'm best at

WORSTS: My worst subjects
              My most hated chores
              My dumbest moments

FAVORITES: My favorite books
              My favorite animals
              My favorite places

 Read a lot. Read books, magazines, and newspapers. Read about things you've never read about before—moon walks, raising rabbits, and so on. Jot down writing ideas as you read.

 Do a lot. Try new things. Join new clubs. Make new friends. The more you do, the more you'll have to write about.

 Write often. Write about your thoughts and experiences in a journal (or in part of your idea notebook). Always check this writing when you're looking for new ideas.

Collecting Details

Once you've chosen a subject to write about, you need to collect details. **Details** are the facts and ideas that make your writing interesting. There are three ways to collect details for your writing:

Collecting Strategies

1. **Gather** facts from books, newspapers, magazines, videos, and CD's.

2. **Talk** to other people about your topic. (See "Learning to Interview," pages 252-255, for help.)

3. **Collect** your thoughts about a topic. Some writers call this *brainstorming*. On the next page, we list different ways to collect your thoughts.

Thinking and Gathering

List Ideas ● Listing is one of the easiest ways to collect ideas. Just write your subject at the top of a piece of paper. Then start listing ideas as they come to mind. Don't worry about how your list looks. Just keep writing down ideas about your subject.

Answer the 5 W's ● Answer these five questions—*Who? What? When? Where?* and *Why?*—to collect ideas.

Make a Cluster or Map ● Clustering, or mapping, is a good way to think about a subject. Clustering helps you organize the ideas that pop into your head. (See page 264 for an example.)

Study Your Subject ● Think about your subject in these ways:

* **Describe the subject.** How does it look, sound, smell, taste, and feel? How does it make you feel?

* **Compare it.** What other things is it like, and how is it like them? What things is it not like?

* **Decide about its value.** What are the best things about it? What are the worst things? What do you like about it and dislike about it?

Use a Collection Sheet ● Collection charts and gathering grids help you keep track of your ideas. (See pages 119 and 148 for examples.)

Planning
and Drafting Guide

You've picked a subject to write about and collected lots of ideas and information. What's next?

Write down four key points.
(They will keep you on track as you write.)

Subject: What or who are you writing about?
Purpose: Why are you writing? To explain? To describe?
Form: What form will you use? A story? A report?
Readers: Who will read your writing?

Key Points for a Personal Story

Subject: The day I won the pinewood derby

Purpose: To describe an exciting day

Form: A personal story

Readers: Classmates

Plan your beginning.

The **beginning** has to tell what you are writing about, and it has to make your readers want to keep reading!

Here are some good ways to begin:

A Surprising Fact

Third graders in Ms. Grayson's class collected 22,000 aluminum cans in just six weeks.

A Quote

"Ouch! A bee stung me!" yelled my little brother Brad.

A Question

Would you ever want to eat 15 worms?

Write your first draft.

* Once you get your first sentence or two on paper, keep writing! Get all of your ideas down, but don't try to write a perfect paper.

* If you get stuck, look at your collecting notes. Also check your four key points.

* When you have written down all of your main ideas, your first draft is done. Good for you! (See page 17 for a sample first draft.)

Revising, Conferencing, and Editing Guide

Revising Your Writing

Do you remember Pinocchio, built by the wood-carver Geppetto? Geppetto cut the wood with care, chiseled here, and sanded there. Finally, Pinocchio looked like a real boy, and actually came to life!

Making Your First Draft Better

A writer is like a wood-carver. You make big changes and little changes until your writing is clear, complete, and interesting. This chapter will tell you how to go about making changes in your writing.

When you take the time to **revise** your writing and bring it to life, you will have something to be proud of—as Geppetto was proud of Pinocchio.

How Do You Get Started?

Read Your Draft to Yourself ● When you're ready to revise, read your first draft two or three times.

* Read it out loud at least once.
* Look for parts that you like and parts that may need work.

Share Your Draft with Friends ● They may have good ideas you didn't think of.

* Ask them which parts they liked.
* Ask them which parts they have questions about.

How Do You Make Changes?

Look at the Main Parts First ● Does your writing have a good beginning, middle, and ending? (See the next page for help.)

Check the Details Next ● Does your writing include a lot of details and describing words? (See page 46 for help.)

Your favorite authors revise their stories many times before they are ready to share them.

Checking the Three Main Parts

Make sure your **beginning** introduces or names your subject in an interesting way.

One way: I have six guppies. *(Makes the point.)*

A better way: **I asked my dad if I could get six pets. He said, "Six! Six of what?" I told him my friend Alex was giving guppies away. Dad said it was okay as long as I took care of them.** *(Interesting!)*

Make sure the **middle** part describes or tells about your subject.

My guppies live in an aquarium that has colored pebbles and plants. I feed them every morning, just a pinch. My fish may be little, but they eat like pigs. Two seconds after I put the food in, it's gone! *(Sounds good!)*

Make sure the **ending** reminds your readers about the subject. (Make the ending as good as your beginning.)

One way: That is all I have to say about my guppies. *(Well, okay.)*

A better way: **I like my guppies a lot. I don't mind taking care of them. I like feeding them and watching them eat.** *(Right on track!)*

Show Don't Tell

One of the most important revising tips to remember is to "show" instead of "tell."

Telling: We had a neat fort. *(Ho-hum.)*

Showing: **Our fort stood on stilts six feet high! It smelled like wood and rope when we crawled inside.** *(Yes!)*

Bringing Your Writing to Life

Here is one way to bring your writing to life with "showing" details:

Use the five senses.

These authors put in details that help us to see and smell a fall day and to hear and feel a thunderstorm.

Everything was golden brown. There was the smell of smoke everywhere, and the smell of leaves burning, and sounds carried a long, long way.

— Willie Morris,
Good Old Boy

When the thunder ROARED above us so hard it shook the windows and rattled the dishes in the cupboards, we just smiled and ate our Thunder Cake.

— Patricia Polacco,
Thunder Cake

(From *Thunder Cake*, © 1990 by Patricia Polacco. Reprinted by permission of Philomel Books.)

Revising Checklist

Do I need to **add** any information?

- [ ] Do I have a good beginning?
- [ ] Have I included all the important details?
- [ ] Do I need to add an ending?

Do I need to **cut** any information?

- [ ] Have I stuck to my topic?
- [ ] Have I repeated myself in some parts?

Do I need to **move** any parts?

- [ ] Are my sentences in the best order?
- [ ] Do any ideas or details seem to be out of place?

Do I need to **rewrite** any parts?

- [ ] Are there ideas or sentences that are unclear?
- [ ] Have I used my five senses?

Conferencing with Partners

Dentists talk about fillings; bus drivers talk about safety. When people who have the same job get together to talk, it's called a **conference**. People share ideas in order to do their jobs better.

You can hold a conference to share ideas about your writing. Maybe you'd like to talk with one other person or with a small group. Your goal is to help one another do your best work. This chapter tells you how to have good writing conferences.

Why talk about your writing?
Conference partners
can help you . . .

* see the strongest parts of your writing,
* get new ideas,
* fix problems, and
* find mistakes.

How to Work with Partners

When you're the writer:

- Have your writing ready to share. You can share your writing at different points during the writing process.
- Tell your partners something about your writing. (But don't say too much.)
- Read your writing aloud.
- Listen to what your partners say about it. (You may not always agree with them, but take time to think about what they say.)

When you're the listener:

- Listen carefully to the writer.
- Jot down a few notes to help you remember ideas.
- Tell the writer something you like about the writing. ("I like the way . . .")
- Ask about things you don't understand. ("What do you mean when you say . . .")
- Be kind. Always talk about the writing in a helpful way. (Say something like this: "Maria, I don't think *ran* is the right word for what that dog did. Do you mean *charged?*")

When to Conference with Partners

You can conference with partners at different steps in the writing process.

During prewriting, conference partners can help you . . .
* choose a subject to write about, and
* think of places to find information.

After your first draft, conference partners can tell you . . .
* what they like, and
* what parts are unclear or out of order.

As you revise, conference partners can tell you if . . .
* your beginning gets their interest,
* your middle sticks to the topic, and
* your ending is good.

As you edit and proofread, conference partners can help you . . .
* find sentence errors,
* choose the right words to use, and
* correct punctuation and spelling errors.

Response Sheets

A **response sheet** has places for you to write comments about a partner's writing. Here are two ideas for response sheets.

Memorable

On the top half of a sheet of paper, write "Memorable." (List things you like about a piece of writing here.)

More

Halfway down the sheet, write "More." (List questions you have or parts that need work here.)

Conference Checklist

Organization:

✔ Does the writing have a beginning, a middle, and an ending?

✔ Are all of the ideas in the best order?

Details:

✔ Do all of the details talk about the subject?

✔ Are there enough details and examples?

Style & Mechanics:

✔ Are the sentences easy to read?

✔ Is the writing free of errors?

Editing
and Proofreading

Editing and **proofreading** help you get your writing ready to share. This step becomes important after you have changed, or revised, the main ideas in your first draft. Editing means making sure that your writing is clear and correct. Proofreading means checking for errors one last time before you share a final copy.

Ask for Help!

It is easy to miss errors when you edit and proofread. So make sure that you ask a classmate or family member to help you. All writers, even your favorite authors, have help during this step in the process. (The checklist on the next page lists all of the things you should check for.)

Editing and Proofing Checklist

Sentences

☐ **Are all of your sentences complete?**
(See pages 69-71 for help.)

☐ **Have you written some longer sentences?**
(See pages 72-73.)

Words

☐ **Did you use interesting words?**

  ✱ Use strong action words (*giggle, slam, cram,* and so on).

  ✱ Use good describing words, too (*bubbly, squishy, tidy,* and so on).

☐ **Have you used the right words** (*one* instead of *won,* or *no* instead of *know*)?
(See pages 318-323 for help.)

Punctuation, Spelling, Capitalization

☐ **Have you put the right end punctuation mark after each sentence?**

☐ **Have you spelled your words correctly?**

☐ **Have you capitalized names and the first word of each sentence?** (See pages 307-309 for help.)

Building Paragraphs

Writing
Paragraphs

Where docs every good sentence belong? In a good paragraph, of course. A **paragraph** is made up of several sentences, all about the same subject. If you put these sentences together in just the right way, they will present a clear and interesting picture of your subject.

What's Ahead?

In this chapter, we'll tell you everything you need to know about paragraphs. We'll name the three basic parts, show you four different kinds of paragraphs, and list the steps in the paragraph-writing process. So let's get started!

SNOW DAY

The Basic Parts of a Paragraph

A paragraph has three parts: the **topic sentence**, the **body** or middle part, and the **closing sentence**. Here's how these three parts make a paragraph.

Topic
sentence

Body

Snow Day!

It snowed a lot yesterday, so school let out early. It started to snow before lunch. At first, a few big flakes came floating down. But then it came down harder and harder. Snow piled up on the playground. At 12:30, the principal announced that school would let out at 1:00. Thanks to the snowstorm, we had a free afternoon!

Closing
sentence

How the Basic Parts Work

A paragraph is like a train. The *topic sentence* is the train's engine. It is the sentence that drives the paragraph. The sentences in the *body* are the boxcars. They carry the cargo—all of the facts and details that tell about the subject. The *closing sentence* is the caboose. It brings the paragraph to an end.

A Closer Look at the Parts

The Topic Sentence ● A good topic sentence does two things: (1) It names the subject. (2) It tells what part of the subject you will talk about. (The part of a subject you talk about is called the *focus*.)

> EXAMPLE:
>
> It snowed a lot yesterday (subject), so school let out early (focus).

The Body ● The sentences in the body explain or describe the subject. All of the ideas in the body should be stated in the best order. To help put things in order, list the main ideas *before* you write your paragraph.

> EXAMPLE: (This list relates to the sample paragraph.)
>
> – It started to snow
> – Big flakes at first
> – Snow piled up
> – Principal closed school early

The Closing Sentence ● The last sentence reminds readers of what the paragraph is about. Or it gives them one last idea to think about.

> EXAMPLE:
>
> Thanks to the snowstorm, we had a free afternoon! (reminds readers about the subject)

Types of Paragraphs

There are four types of paragraphs: **narrative, descriptive, expository,** and **persuasive.** Each one does something different.

Narrative Paragraph

A **narrative** paragraph tells a story about an event in the writer's life. As you read this model by Patrick Brede, watch for details that make the story interesting and real.

Cooking with Grandma

Topic sentence ⟶ My grandma and I had so much fun cooking in our backyard. First, we'd start by filling empty yogurt containers with little twigs and all

Interesting details ⟶ sorts of leaves. These were some of our vegetables. We also used bits of grass for cabbage. Then we'd stir our food with sticks and set it in the sun to cook. We checked our dinner all the time. Sometimes we would sprinkle everything with sand for salt and pepper.

Closing sentence ⟶ Finally, we would have a big feast!

Descriptive Paragraph

A **descriptive** paragraph describes a person, place, or thing. A good descriptive paragraph uses words that help readers *see, hear, smell, feel,* and *taste* the subject. As you read the model by Natalie Stern, watch for good descriptive words.

Zev's Deli

Zev's Deli is one of my favorite ← ·· Topic sentence
places to visit. When you walk in the
door, you smell corned beef and fresh
coffee and 100 other great smells. ← ·· Details giving smells, sights, and sounds
There are shelves everywhere, crammed
with all kinds of food. There's olive oil in
tin containers, pickles in jars, and boxes ←
and boxes of crackers. You can hear ←
Zev yelling out people's names when
their food is ready. My favorite thing to ← ·· Best detail saved for last
order is cheese blintzes. They taste soft
and sweet and warm. Zev puts bright
red strawberry sauce on my blintzes.
Yum!

Expository Paragraph

An **expository** paragraph explains something or gives information. It includes all the facts a reader needs to understand the subject. As you read this model by Tim Green, watch for words that explain.

Living with a Little Brother

Topic sentence ·········►   Living with my little brother can be hard. First, he tries to copy me. If I have a second glass of milk, he does, too.
Examples explaining the subject   Second, he always wants to play with my friends. If we play basketball, he wants to join in. But he is too small. Third, he wants to stay up as long as I do. He always says to my mom, "But Tim gets to stay up later." My mom says that he looks up to
Closing idea ·········►   me, and I should be proud about that. I'm trying to be, but it is not always easy.

TIP: In expository paragraphs, time words (*first, second, third*) are used to keep the main ideas in order.

Persuasive Paragraph

A **persuasive** paragraph tells your opinion about something. It also tries to get your readers to agree with you. As you read the model by Susan Rodigou, watch for reasons that make the writer's opinion strong.

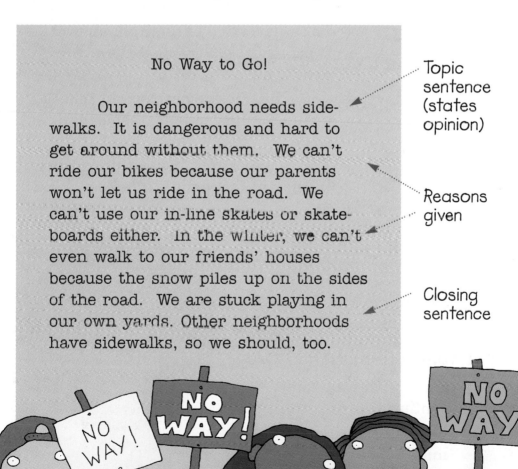

No Way to Go!

Our neighborhood needs sidewalks. It is dangerous and hard to get around without them. We can't ride our bikes because our parents won't let us ride in the road. We can't use our in-line skates or skateboards either. In the winter, we can't even walk to our friends' houses because the snow piles up on the sides of the road. We are stuck playing in our own yards. Other neighborhoods have sidewalks, so we should, too.

Topic
sentence
(states
opinion)

Reasons
given

Closing
sentence

Writing a Paragraph

Prewriting
Planning Your Writing

Select a Subject ● Choose an interesting subject.

Collect Details ● Gather your facts and examples.

* For a narrative paragraph, answer *who? what? when? where?* and *why?* about your subject.

* For a descriptive paragraph, collect sights, sounds, smells, tastes, and so on.

* For an expository paragraph, gather important facts and examples.

* For a persuasive paragraph, list reasons that support your opinion.

Writing the First Draft

Put Your Information in Order

* Start with your topic sentence.

* Explain the subject in the middle sentences (the body).

* Sum everything up in the closing sentence.

Revising
Improving
Your Writing

Check Your First Draft ● Look closely at each part—the topic sentence, the body, and the closing.

    ✻ Are your sentences clear and in the best order?

    ✻ Do you need to add more details about your subject? (Check the models on pages 58-61 for help.)

Editing
and
Proofing

Correct Your Writing ● Use these questions as a guide when you check your revised writing for errors:

    ✻ Are your words interesting and colorful (*soft* or *sweet* instead of *good*)?

    ✻ Have you used the right words (*know* instead of *no*), and are your words spelled correctly?

    ✻ Does each of your sentences begin with a capital letter and end with the correct punctuation mark?

Writing a Summary

You learn a lot from reading chapters in books and articles in magazines or encyclopedias. Sometimes you must share the information in a special project or report. Writing a summary is a handy way to do this.

Panning for Gold

A **summary** contains the most important ideas from your reading. You sift out the golden nuggets, or main ideas, and leave the rest behind. Then you combine your thoughts into a clear paragraph.

This chapter will show you a model summary, plus guidelines for writing your own.

Article

Read this article about the earth. Then study the model summary. The summary includes only main ideas.

Our Earth: Sphere of Land and Water

Astronauts looking down at the earth from space see a **sphere** that looks like a beautiful globe. About one-fourth of the earth's surface is land. The rest, about three-fourths of the total surface, is water.

The largest bodies of water are the **oceans**. The oceans are not really separate bodies of water, but one great ocean. This great ocean is divided into four parts: the Pacific Ocean, Atlantic Ocean, Indian Ocean, and the Arctic Ocean.

The land on the surface of the earth is divided into **continents**: North America, South America, Europe, Asia, Africa, Antarctica, and Australia. The continents float in the one great ocean like islands.

MODEL Summary

The earth is a sphere made up of land and water. There's a lot more water than land. The largest bodies of water are the four oceans, which are really one big ocean! The land is divided into continents that float like islands in the one great ocean.

Prewriting
Planning
Your Writing

Writing a Summary

Read Carefully ● Learn as much as you can about the reading assignment.

* Read the assignment once to get the general meaning. Then read it again, more closely. Study key words in *italics* or **boldface**.

* Next, find the main ideas and list them on your paper. (See the steps below for help.)

How to Find Main Ideas

1. Check the title. The most important idea is often there.

2. Look at the first and last sentences of every paragraph.

3. Watch for key words in *italics* or **boldface**.

Writing the First Draft

Write Clear Sentences ● Use your own words, except for key words.

* Your first sentence should tell the most important idea.
* In the rest of your summary, include the other main ideas.

Revising
Improving Your Writing

Read and Review ● Ask the following questions.

* Are my sentences clear?
* Have I included all the important ideas?
* Are the ideas in the best order?
* Have I put in too many details?

Editing and Proofing

Check for Errors ● Check your spelling, capitalization, and punctuation. Then write a neat final copy to share.

Building Sentences

Writing Basic

Sentences

Does "I broccoli" make sense? No, something is missing. Does "I love broccoli" sound any better? It should (even if you don't like broccoli). The second example states a complete thought.

Making Sense

A group of words that states a complete thought is called a **sentence**. We use sentences in our writing. We use sentences when we talk to other people. And we read them in our favorite stories and books. In other words, we use sentences all the time. What do you need to know about sentences to use them well? Review the next two pages to find out. (Also see pages 324-327.)

SENTENCE Parts

Subject

All sentences have a subject and a verb. The **subject** names who or what is doing something.

Jamie draws dinosaurs.

subject

Verb (Predicate)

The **verb** tells the action of the sentence.

Jamie draws dinosaurs.

verb

There is another kind of verb called a *linking verb*. Instead of telling an action, a linking verb links the subject to another part of the sentence.

Dinosaurs are awesome.

linking verb

TIP: Remember, a sentence is not complete unless it has a subject and a verb.

Other Words

Most sentences have other words that help complete the idea.

other words

Jamie draws dinosaurs on huge pieces of paper.

SENTENCE Problems

▶ A **fragment** happens when you forget an important part of the sentence.

Fragment: Gave her dog a bath. (A subject is missing.)

Corrected Sentence:
Sarah gave her dog a bath.

▶ A **run-on** happens when you run two sentences together.

Run-On: Mickey looked funny he was one big mess of bubbles. (This example is really two sentences.)

Corrected Sentences:
Mickey looked funny. He was one big mess of bubbles.

▶ A **rambling** sentence happens when an idea goes on and on.

Rambling Sentence: Mickey jumped out of the tub and he shook water over everything and Sarah got mad and she ran after him. (Too many *and's* are used.)

Corrected Sentences:
Mickey jumped out of the tub. He shook water over everything. Sarah got mad, and she ran after him.

Combining Sentences

Sentence combining is making one longer sentence out of two or more shorter sentences. Here's an example:

Three Shorter Sentences:

Heather likes slithery snakes.
She likes skittery chameleons.
She likes warty toads.

One Longer Sentence:

Heather likes slithery snakes, skittery chameleons, and warty toads.

Why Combine?

Combining sentences helps you write longer sentences. Longer sentences can make your writing more interesting and easier to read. You can learn how to combine sentences on the next page.

Combine with a Series ● You can combine short sentences that tell different things about the same subject.

> The desert is hot.
> The desert is sunny.
> The desert is dry.

The desert is <u>hot, sunny,</u> and <u>dry.</u>

Combine with Key Words ● You can add a key word from one sentence to another sentence.

> My mom went to Japan. She went yesterday.

My mom went to Japan <u>yesterday.</u>

TIP: Sometimes you can put a key word like "yesterday" at the beginning of your new sentence. That's a good way to keep all your sentences from starting the same way.

Combine with Compound Subjects ● A compound subject is two or more subjects in one sentence.

> Carlos speaks Spanish.
> Gaby speaks Spanish.

<u>Carlos</u> and <u>Gaby</u> speak Spanish.

Combine with Compound Verbs ● A compound verb is two or more verbs in one sentence.

> Gaby wrote a poem in Spanish.
> Gaby published the poem.

Gaby <u>wrote</u> and <u>published</u> a poem in Spanish.

2 The Forms of Writing

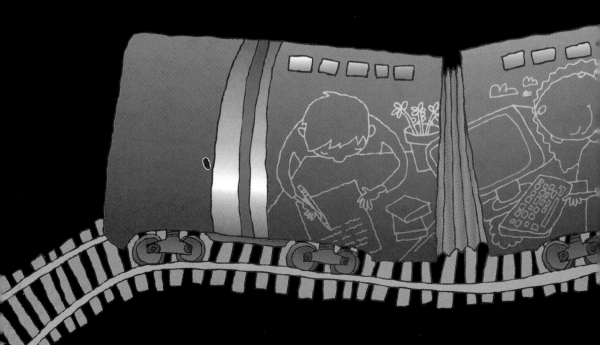

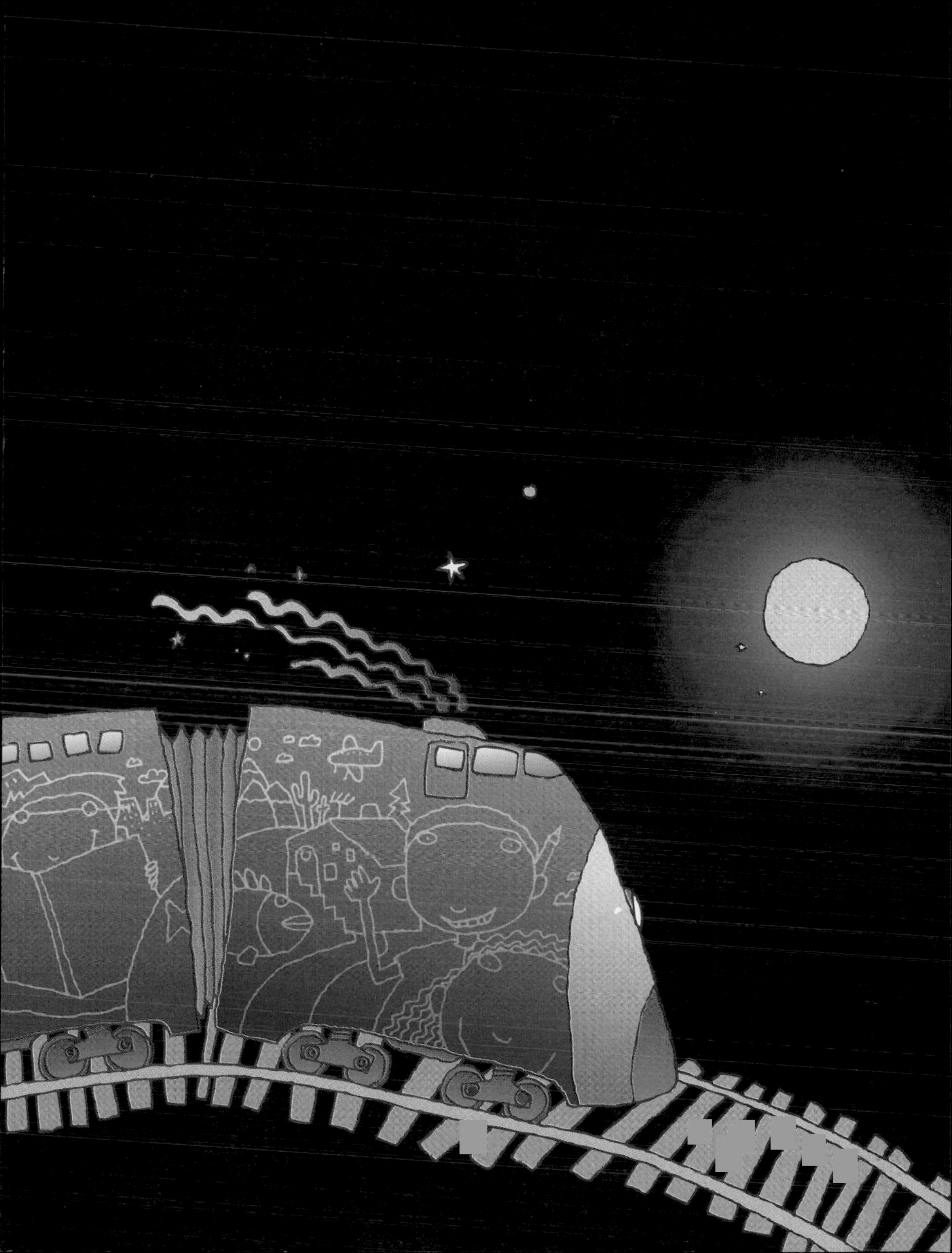

Personal Writing

Writing in Journals

Your favorite authors never stop writing. Stories, magazine articles, letters—they do it all. Most of them also keep special notebooks, or **journals**, to write about interesting things they see or learn during each day. Writing in a journal gives them ideas for stories.

Your Turn

You can write in a journal just as well as anybody else (including your favorite authors). You read and learn new things. You have ideas pop into your head. You see stuff happening. Writing in a journal helps you think about all of these things. On the next few pages, you can learn about three kinds of journals.

Writing in a Personal Journal

A **personal journal** is your own special place to write about anything and everything. You can . . .

▶ write about interesting things you see and hear,

▶ collect ideas for stories and poems,

▶ remember happy (and not so happy) times,

▶ and write secret letters and notes.

Writing About Something You Hear

Missy's grandmother told her about going to school in England. Missy wrote in her journal to remember things.

March 13

In Grandma's school, everyone had to learn to swim. They even tested you on swimming, and it was hard! She said England is an island, so the teachers wanted everyone to know how to swim. She also said that girls and boys had to play on different playgrounds. She only had one good dress for school!

Writing in a Reading Journal

A **reading journal** is a place to write about the stories and books you read. Is something exciting? Sad? Scary? Is there a funny part you want to remember? Is there a big word you want to write down? Do you have any questions about your reading? You can write about these ideas in your journal.

Write a few lines or many lines. Use complete sentences or brief notes. The choice is yours. For examples, look below at what Jamie, Dave, and Marisa wrote about.

Student MODELS

Fun/No Fun by James Stevenson

The author says cowboy boots and cookies with raisins are fun. Galoshes [snow boots] and cookies with no raisins are no fun. He's right!
— Jamie

Macho Nacho and Other Rhyming Riddles by Giulo Maestro

This is a funny book! "What do you call pasta for pooches?" NOODLES FOR POODLES Ha! Ha!
—Dave

Water by Kim Taylor

So salt can make an egg float? Why is that? I'm not sure I really understand. Salt must do something to the water. Maybe it makes it heavier.

—Marisa

Writing in a Learning Log

A **learning log**, or class journal, is a place for you to write about your subjects—language arts, math, science, and social studies. You can ask questions, write interesting facts, list new words, and so on.

Student MODELS

Thinking About New Ideas ● Melinda's teacher had asked the class, "What is multiplication?" Here's what Melinda wrote in her learning log:

It is a lot like addition. Once I bought my dad 4 boxes of golf balls. Each box had 3 balls in it. That was 12 new balls. You can get the answer in two ways.

$$3 + 3 + 3 + 3 = 12$$
$$3 \times 4 = 12$$

Observing ● Charlie was supposed to practice looking at something. He chose his left shoe.

1. made by Nike
2. made in China
3. white and black
4. dirty
5. 2 holes
6. orange shoelace
7. size $5^1/_2$
8. curling at the toe

Asking Questions ● Rosie listened to her teacher talk about Abraham Lincoln. She thought about important questions about his childhood.

How did Abe Lincoln feel when his father got married again? How did his life change?

Learning with Pictures

You can also draw pictures or diagrams in a learning log, like this drawing by Billie. He was studying the digestive system in his science class.

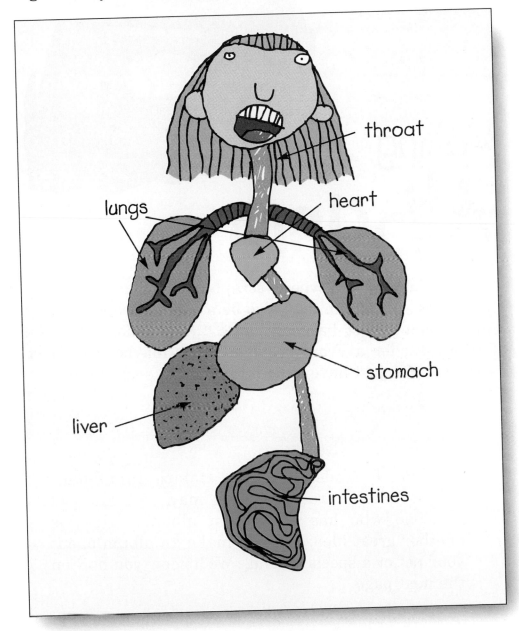

Making Albums

An **album** is a type of scrapbook—a place for special memories. An album may also be a place to collect things. Maybe you collect baseball cards. (I'll trade you a Ken Griffey, Jr., for a Frank Thomas.) Or maybe you collect stickers. You just have to be interested in something.

Kinds of Albums

Some students collect stamps in albums. Others collect rare coins. You may even know of someone who has a vacation album. Here is another great idea: You can make an album about your pet or a special friend. We'll show you how on the next page.

Making a Pet or Best Friend Album

Getting Started ● A good way to start an album like this is with a picture of your pet or friend. You can use a photograph, or you can draw a picture yourself. Then write something interesting or funny under it.

Moving On ● Here are other ideas for your album:

* Facts about your pet or friend (age, fur or hair color, eye color, size, and so on)
* When and how you met
* Things you like to do together
* Things your pet or friend loves or hates
* Strange or surprising facts about your pet or friend

Putting It Together ● The ideas listed here will help you put your album together.

✔ **Make** a neat and colorful cover for your album.

✔ **Organize** all of your information so it follows a pattern. (You may want to organize the different pages in your album by first memories, middle memories, and last memories.)

✔ **Place** the pictures and words on each page so they are fun to look at and read.

✔ **Treat** your album with special care.

Writing Lists

Moms, dads, mayors, mechanics, coaches, cooks—everyone writes **lists**. Lists make jobs a little easier to complete. Take a look at the shopping list a zookeeper made to feed 10 animals. (These must be *mega*-animals.)

800 pounds alfalfa
30 pounds apples
25 loaves bread
30 pounds carrots
25 pounds potatoes
60 pounds fish

How Lists Help You

Lists can help you remember things, collect ideas for writing, think in different ways, or just have fun. The next three pages will show you how to do all of these things. Once you start listing, you won't want to stop!

1. Remembering Things

What do you need to remember? Things to do at home? Supplies for school? Just make a list. Sean made a list of the things he needed for his pond-life project:

glue
colored paper
tape
colored pencils
string
crayons
tissue scraps

2. Collecting Ideas for Writing

During one cold winter, students in Troy, New York, made a long list of winter words. They listened for winter words on radio and TV, and looked for them in the newspaper. After two weeks, they had a list of 50 different ways to say or show, "It's cold!" Here are just a few:

snow, ice, slush, freezing rain, icicle, blizzard, howling wind, Brrr! . . .

These students used their word list to write tall tales about winter. They also wrote personal stories about a winter experience. List making gave them good ideas for their writing projects!

3. Thinking in Different Ways

Lists can help us open our minds to new thoughts. There is a book for adults called *14,000 Things to Be Happy About*. The writers of this book thought about being happy in many different ways. Here are some of the things listed in this book:

* seeing the moon rise
* a baseball game going extra innings
* Bugs Bunny
* (plus 13,997 more things to be happy about!)

Students Try It Out ● Students in Beaufort, South Carolina, made their own list of 100 things that make them happy. They wrote their list on a poster and hung it up in their classroom. Here are five of the things listed:

*eating pancakes
riding a bike
staying over with a friend
fishing with Dad
cooking with Grandma*

4. Having Fun

The poet Jack Prelutsky likes to have fun with his poetry. In one of his poems, he lists all the strange things that Sadie Snatt liked to eat:

> *I sup on slugs and soft-boiled bugs*
> *and tasty toads on toast,*
> *on donkey tongues and monkey lungs*
> *and caterpillar roast, . . .*

(The four lines from "Sadie Snatt" in *The Sheriff of Rottenshot* by Jack Prelutsky, © 1992, are reprinted by permission of Greenwillow Books, a division of William Morrow and Company, Inc.)

A Student's Shopping List ● To have fun, Rodney, wrote a shopping list from A to Z for a hippopotamus:

A apples

B bananas

C chocolate cakes

D donut holes

E eggplants

F french fries

The list ends with zucchinis. Can you guess what comes in between french fries and zucchinis? Try.

NEXT STOP Make your own shopping list. Buy 10, 20, 30, or however many items you need. Shop for yourself, your little brother, your favorite animal, an old troll, or anyone else. Shop for yummy foods, yucky foods, or foods no one has heard of before. (And have fun.)

Writing Friendly Notes

Has anyone ever given you a note? Maybe Mom or Dad left a note in your lunch box. Maybe your teacher gave you a note about your report. Maybe your best friend wrote you a secret note.

Short and Quick

Notes are different from letters because they are fast and easy to write. Plus, you don't have to address an envelope or find a stamp! You just hand a note to someone, or put it where the person will find it. The fun starts when you get a note back!

Great Reasons to Send Notes

You can send a friendly note at any time and for any reason. Think about these reasons:

To Say Thank You

Has someone done something special for you? Is there someone you really should thank? Tell them so in a note.

Dear Bobby-Anne,
Thanks so much for finding my snake. You are the best school custodian in the world!
Brian

To Ask a Favor

Do you need help learning a new game or working on a project? Most people like to be helpers and are happy to be asked.

Dear Joe,
I'm glad you're in my class this year. I hope you will show me how you can kick a soccer ball so high.
I read a funny riddle: Do you know where the three little pigs went on vacation? To New Hampshire. (Get it?)

Your friend,
Mike

To Send a Special Message

Sometimes it's important to tell a friend that he or she is special.

Dear Sara,

Last weekend we went to a wildlife park. One part had all these birds. I thought of you because I know you love birds.

Your friend,
Maria

To Share Something You Know

Friends enjoy hearing something new or interesting. So tell them in a note.

Hey J,

Did you see the fun book Mr. Halley brought to class? Here's my favorite joke in it:

Teacher: Why can a person's hand never be longer than 11 inches?

Student: Because if it were 12 inches, it would be a foot.

See you after school,
Will

(Joke from *Funny You Should Ask.* Text copyright © 1992 by Marvin Terban. Reprinted by permission of Clarion Books/Houghton Mifflin Co. All rights reserved.)

Fun Note Ideas

1. Use (or make your own) special paper.

2. Decorate your note with a picture.

3. Add some special touch to make your note interesting. (Use a secret code, add a riddle, and so on.)

Susie,
This star is for you. Can you guess why?
          Ms. Carey

Ari,
Let's get together after school.

Teddy

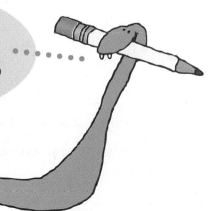

Dear Blue Eyes,

Open the clock's face. That's when we'll meet. See ya.

Lonestar

at 2:15 P.M.

Try writing a note to someone who isn't your special friend. You may start a new friendship that way.

Writing Friendly Letters

It's fun to write a **friendly letter**, and even more fun to receive one. Letters keep us in touch with faraway friends and relatives. They can also put us in touch with someone we admire, like a sports hero or an author.

Parts of a Friendly Letter

Friendly letters have five parts: *the heading, the salutation, the body, the closing,* and *the signature.*

1 The **heading** includes your address and the date.

2 The **salutation**, or greeting, usually begins with the word "Dear" and is followed by the name of the person you are writing to. Place a comma after the name.

3 The **body** of the letter contains your thoughts and ideas.

4 The **closing** can be anything from "Love" to "See you soon." Follow the closing with a comma.

5 Put your **signature** below your closing.

Student MODEL

Andrea Curé wrote to Ms. Nathan, her third-grade teacher who had moved away. Ms. Nathan had sent Andrea a picture along with her letter.

1 1256 Cherry Street
Troy, MI 48003
June 2, 1995

Dear Ms. Nathan, **2**

You put hearts in the envelope!

You look great in the picture! Wow, traveling to Yosemite Park sounds cool. And it's nice you and Dr. **3** Nathan are doing something special every weekend.

That's great that you are playing the Mozart Concerto in C, even though you are playing an easy version. Yes! I am proud of you. I am in Level 3 in piano.

Morse School is really looking great. They are almost done remodeling. I wish you could see it. I think we'll get to move back in soon.

My new teacher is Ms. Porter. Many of the kids you had last year are in Ms. Porter's class.

Please write back and tell me more about California.

4 Fondly,
Andrea **5**

P.S. We had a lot of snow, about 17 inches.

Prewriting
Planning Your Writing

Writing a Letter

Pick Someone to Write To ● Maybe your best friend has moved away, and you miss him. Or maybe you would like to write to a favorite grown-up. Then there are all those famous people you admire.

Plan What You Will Say ● Make a short list of the things you want to say. Todd's list for a letter to his friend Manny looked like this:

* new school year
* friends
* baseball results
* Manny's new home

Writing the First Draft

Include Your Best Ideas ●
Pick one idea from your list to get you started. Then keep adding ideas and details until you say everything.

Revising
Improving Your Writing

Review Your Work ● Keep in mind, you won't be there to explain yourself when the person gets your letter. So make sure it is clear and complete.

* Do I need to explain anything better?
* Does my letter have interesting details?

Editing and Proofing

Check for Errors ● Review your letter for careless mistakes.

* Check for spelling and punctuation errors.
* Write a neat final copy to send.
* Make sure you have correctly addressed the envelope.

When we write to people we know very well, we can add personal touches like doodles or little pictures.

Writing Personal Narratives

On the way to school, do you ever say to a friend, "Guess what happened"? Of course you do. Everyone likes telling personal stories. It's as important to you and me as cheese pizza and summer vacation. These stories are called **personal narratives**.

From Telling to Writing

This chapter will show you how to write personal narratives so they sound just as exciting as the ones you tell. First read the student model on the next page. Then begin your own story. (Follow the steps listed on pages 98-99.)

TIP: You'll never run out of ideas for personal narratives. Each day brings new experiences.

Student MODEL

Here is a personal narrative written by Adam Kendall.

Something's There

Last February, my dad and I were pulling down an old chicken coop in our backyard. I ripped off a board and saw something.

"What's that?" I said.

"It's just a pile of old gray rags," my dad said.

Then I yanked off another board and saw something pink and squishy-looking.

"Dad, can gray rags have a pink nose?"

Finally, Dad looked carefully into the chicken coop. "It's a possum! We just woke up a sleeping possum."

The possum walked away like it was dizzy. Then it disappeared into the woods. Dad laughed and I did, too.

Prewriting
Planning
Your Writing

Writing a Personal Narrative

List Topic Ideas ● Make a list of different things that have happened to you. Include happy, funny, proud, strange, and important events.

Select One Idea ● Circle one idea in your list that interests you the most. If you can answer *yes* to the questions below, then you've selected a great idea to write about.

* Do I have strong feelings (happy or sad) about this event?

* Can I remember how things looked, sounded, and felt?

* Would I really like to share this story with others?

Plan Your Writing ● List everything that happened in this event. (Or draw simple pictures of everything instead, like a comic strip.)

Writing the First Draft

Write with Feeling ● Write your narrative as if you were telling this story to your best friend. Make your story exciting!

* Use words like *first* and *next* to help readers follow your story.

* Use words that help your reader know how things looked and sounded:

I saw something pink and squishy-looking.

* Use the real words people said:

"Dad, can gray rags have a pink nose?"

Revising
Improving Your Writing

Read and Revise ● Read your first draft out loud. Make sure you have included all of the important points. Also check to see that your ideas are clear and in the right order.

Editing and Proofing

Check for Errors ● Check each sentence for spelling and punctuation errors. Then write a neat final copy of your story to share with your classmates.

Writing Family Stories

Many families have stories they like to tell over and over. Kevin Lewis laughs every time someone tells the story about his uncle eating 17 pancakes. Jenna Bishop always asks her grandfather to tell the story about when he was eleven years old and drove his family from Maine to Arizona.

Sharing Parts of Life

Family stories come in all shapes and sizes. Some stories can be told in a few lines. Others may go on forever. These stories are an important part of life. They show how families can be brave, funny, or strong. This chapter will show you how to write family stories that come alive for readers.

Student MODELS

Pass the Pancakes

Once my uncle ate 17 pancakes! My father bet Uncle Pete he could eat more, but got sick after 14. Later, my father said he should have skipped the syrup. My mother was mad. She said, "Grown men should know better!"

Every time we have pancakes, I think of my uncle. I think of my father, too. I use strawberry jam, but I can only eat four.

On the Road

Would you believe an eleven-year-old boy drove from Maine to Arizona? My grandfather did! His father had died and his mother wanted to move. She didn't know how to drive and said she was too nervous to learn. So her brother taught Grandpa, and he drove the whole way.

Grandpa said the worst part was listening to everybody complain. His seven-year-old sister kept crying, "It's not fair. I want a turn." His five-year-old brother kept crying, "I'm going to be sick." His mother kept yelling, "Watch out!" I keep asking Grandpa to teach me to drive. My dad says, "No way!" Grandpa says, "Wait until you're eleven."

Prewriting
**Planning
Your Writing**

Writing a Family Story

Read and Remember ● Think of family stories related to the ideas listed below. For example, Kevin would have remembered Uncle Pete eating pancakes after thinking about "food."

animals   tricks   food   games
holidays visits   trips   school days

Select a Story ● Choose your favorite family story to write about. Jot down names and details to make sure that you remember the story. (Or ask someone to repeat it for you.)

Writing
the First
Draft

Begin with an Exciting Idea ● Kevin started his story with a wild fact: "Once my uncle ate 17 pancakes!"

Put in Details ● In her story, Jenna added details to tell just what the trip was like. She included information about a crying sister, a sick brother, and a nervous mother.

Revising
Improving
Your Writing

Review Your First Draft ● Listen for things to change as you read.

* Did you forget any important details?
* Are any sentences hard to read?
* Would one of the sentences sound better in a different place?

Share Your Writing ● Get together with a group of classmates and read your stories out loud. Listen carefully so you can tell each other what you like and what you wonder about. You may get some good ideas for making your story even better.

Editing
and
Proofing

Check for Errors ● Make sure all of your sentences are clear. Does each one begin with a capital letter and end with a period, an exclamation point, or a question mark? Also check for spelling errors. Then write a neat copy of your story.

Subject Writing

Writing Alphabet Books

Have you ever had fun with this jump-rope jingle?

A   My name is Alice and my husband's name is Al.
We come from Alabama and we sell apples.

B   My name is Barbara and my husband's name is Bill.
We come from Buffalo and we sell bananas.

When you write a funny jingle or list interesting information in ABC order, you are writing an **alphabet book**.

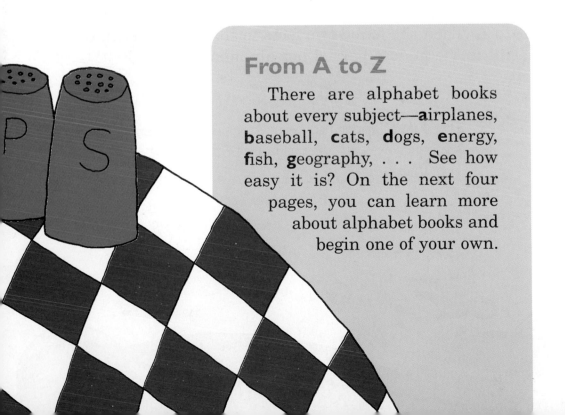

From A to Z

There are alphabet books about every subject—**a**irplanes, **b**aseball, **c**ats, **d**ogs, **e**nergy, **f**ish, **g**eography, . . . See how easy it is? On the next four pages, you can learn more about alphabet books and begin one of your own.

Student MODELS

Here are parts of two alphabet books. Charles organized his book by finding a dinosaur for each letter. He gave the same types of facts for each dinosaur.

A Dinosaur ABC

ALLOSAURUS MEANS "DIFFERENT LIZARD." THIS DINOSAUR WAS 34 FEET LONG AND WEIGHED 4 TONS. IT WAS A MEAT EATER.

BRACHIOSAURUS MEANS "ARM LIZARD." IT WAS 85 FEET LONG. IT WEIGHED 70 TONS AND WAS A PLANT EATER.

CETIOSAURUS MEANS "WHALE LIZARD." IT WAS 45 FEET LONG AND WEIGHED 10 TONS. IT WAS A PLANT EATER.

Julie found 26 names of things in outer space—from A to Z. Then she found two facts to share about each thing. (This is the middle part of her alphabet book.)

An Outer Space ABC

 The **Little Dipper** has seven stars and is shaped like a dipper. The North Star is part of the handle.

 The **Milky Way** galaxy has billions of stars. The earth and sun are part of the Milky Way galaxy.

 A **nebula** is a giant cloud of gas and dust. Stars and planets are born in a nebula.

Prewriting
Planning
Your Writing

Writing an Alphabet Book

Select a Subject ● Think of a subject with lots of examples or parts, like *dinosaurs* or *airplanes*.

List Related Topics ● Make a list of topics, A to Z, about your subject. Charles started listing the names of different dinosaurs for his book.

Study Your Topics ● Learn as much as you can about your topics. Write down notes as you read and learn.

Writing the First Draft

Select the Facts ● Give the same type and number of facts for each topic.
Charles gave the meaning of each dinosaur name. He also told about each dinosaur's size and eating habits. Julie gave two important facts for each of her outer-space topics.

State Your Ideas Clearly ● Write interesting sentences for each topic.

Revising
Improving Your Writing

Read and Review ● Make sure that you have stated the same types of facts for each topic. Also make sure that all of your sentences are clear.

Check for Errors ● Check the spelling of each of your topics. Also check your sentences for capital letters and punctuation marks.

Plan Your Final Copy ● Decide how the final copy of your book will look. Are you going to include pictures and other extras? Are you going to design your book on a computer? (See page 33 for bookmaking directions.)

Editing and Proofing

Make your alphabet book as exciting and interesting as you can!

Writing Zany Alphabet Books

Here's how Jackie planned her zany alphabet book.

Her First Step ● First she made three ABC lists.

People's Names	Words That Mean "To Like"	Names of Flowers
Anna	adores	Queen Anne's Lace
Billy	brags	Begonias
Chris	cares	Clover

Her Next Step ● Then she wrote a sentence using her "A" words for her "A" page, her "B" words for her "B" page, and so on. On each page, she drew the flower to match.

> Jackie's ABC's of Flowers
> Anna adores Queen Anne's Lace.
> Billy brags about Begonias.
> Chris cares about Clover.

NEXT STOP Think of a fun idea for an alphabet book. How about a food alphabet book? *Annie ate an Artichoke.* Or how about a geography book? *Buzz boated to Bermuda.* Or a creepy crawler book? *Cory carried a Caterpillar.*

Writing Newspaper
Stories

Recently, one class started their own newspaper called the *Express*. It included many news stories and human interest stories.

A **news story** reports on an important event. One news story in the *Express* reported on a recycling drive. A **human interest story** reports on a topic that students will find interesting. One story in the *Express* told about students and their pets.

Stating Your Feelings

Another part of the students' newspaper printed letters to the editor. A **letter to the editor** states the writer's feelings about an important topic. You can learn more about all three types of newspaper stories on the pages that follow.

MODEL News Story

THE EXPRESS

1 Room 202 Collects 22,000 Cans in Recycling Drive

by Jesse Murino **2**

3 The students in Ms. Grayson's class collected 22,000 aluminum cans in just six weeks. They asked parents to donate cans, and they found some themselves. The $1,200 from the can recycling will be used to buy trees for the south side of the school yard.

4 "The children did a great job," said Patricia Gomez, school principal. "In years to come, people will look at the trees and remember these children."

Students felt bad when the budget for planting trees was cut. They tried to think of ways to raise money. Sam Jensen had the idea of collecting cans. Everyone thought it was a good idea.

Ms. Grayson said, "I'm proud of these students for working hard to make the future better." **5**

Parts of a News Story

1 The **headline** tells what the story is about.

2 The **byline** shows who wrote the story.

3 The **lead** tells the reader the most important facts.

4 The **body** contains more information about the story.

5 The **ending** gives the reader something to remember.

Writing a News Story

Prewriting
Planning Your Writing

Choose a Topic ● Write about an important event in your school or community.

* Have you taken a field trip?
* Did your class just finish an important project?
* Is your community planning a new park?

Collect Facts ● Here are three ways to collect information for your news story:

* Interviewing You can ask different people questions about your topic.

* Observing You can study your topic very carefully and describe what you see and hear.

* Reading You can read about your topic to understand it better.

News stories usually answer the 5 W's (*who? what? when? where?* and *why?*). Find answers to these questions when you collect information.

Write the Lead ● The first sentence or two in the story is called the **lead**. The lead in your story should give important facts about a topic.

> The students in Ms. Grayson's class **(who)** collected 22,000 aluminum cans **(what)** in just six weeks **(when)**.

Write the Main Part ● The main part of your story should state more facts and ideas about the topic.

> **More Facts** The $1,200 from the can recycling will be used to buy trees for the south side of the school yard.

Write the Ending ● Your ending should say something that helps readers remember the story.

> Ms. Grayson said, "I'm proud of these students for working hard to make the future better."

Revising and Editing

Check Your Work ● Make sure you have answered the 5 W's in your story. Also make sure you have spelled all names correctly.

Human Interest Story

Some students in Ms. Angelo's class took a poll. They asked fourth graders what kinds of pets they had. Then the class wrote a human interest story about this poll.

MODEL Story

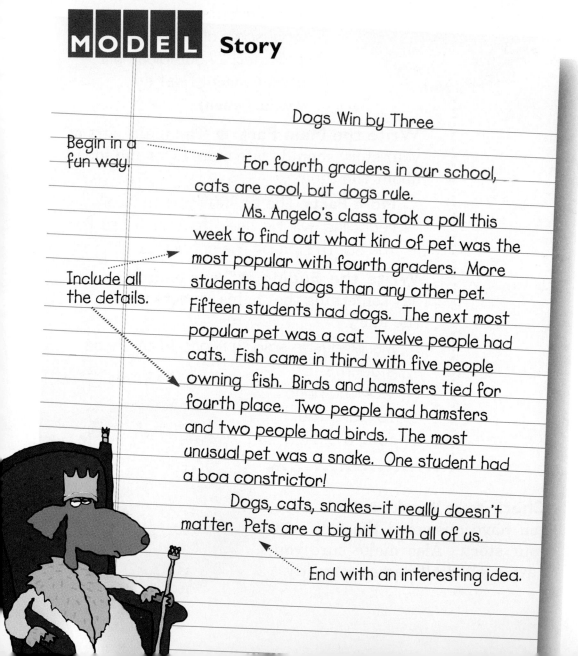

Dogs Win by Three

Begin in a fun way.

For fourth graders in our school, cats are cool, but dogs rule.

Ms. Angelo's class took a poll this week to find out what kind of pet was the most popular with fourth graders. More students had dogs than any other pet. Fifteen students had dogs. The next most popular pet was a cat. Twelve people had cats. Fish came in third with five people owning fish. Birds and hamsters tied for fourth place. Two people had hamsters and two people had birds. The most unusual pet was a snake. One student had a boa constrictor!

Include all the details.

Dogs, cats, snakes—it really doesn't matter. Pets are a big hit with all of us.

End with an interesting idea.

Letter to the Editor

One of your freedoms is the right to state your feelings about important topics. You can practice this right by writing letters to the editor of your newspaper.

 **Letter**

October 12, 1995

Editor
The Express
Granger School
Charlotte, VT   05445

State your feelings.

Dear Editor:
      Third graders need the school library to stay open longer. In third grade, we are beginning to write reports, and we need to use the library after school.
      Five parents have said they would work in the library after school. Many fourth graders at Granger would like the library open longer, too. Fourth-grader Gadi McBride said, "If the library stayed open, we could practice our computer skills."
      We would like this topic discussed at the next teachers' meeting.

Give important facts.

Ask for action.

Thank you,

Uri Levanon
Uri Levanon, Third Grade

Writing Book Reviews

Everyone in Room 14 loves book review time! Students who have written reviews love to share their ideas, and the other kids like hearing about new books.

Sharing Your Feelings

In a **book review**, you can say exactly how you feel about a book. Is the book so good you wanted to stay up late to finish it? Does your book make you laugh or think hard? Do you love the main character? Is there a lot of action?

This chapter will help you write great book reviews. It includes everything from ideas for getting started to student models to tips for writing.

Getting Started

Book reviews usually answer three questions:

 What is the book about?

 Why do I like this book?

What main idea did the author share?

Student

Here's how David Magiera answered these questions in his review of a nonfiction (true) book.

Two Orphan Cubs

 <u>Two Orphan Cubs</u> by Erika Kors is a true story about two bear cubs. One day their mother left them forever. Gary Alt found the cubs in the den. They were very hungry and lonely. Gary put the li'tle bears into a sack and brought the bears to Molly's den. Molly was a bear and had two of her own cubs.

This is a great story. I liked it because there was a happy ending.

Erika Kors did me a favor by writing this book. I learned that people can REALLY save animals' lives!

Writing a Book Review

Prewriting
Planning Your Writing

Select a Book ● Choose a book you are interested in. An adventure story, a fantasy, a sports book—it doesn't matter.

Collect Ideas ● Use the questions on the next page to collect ideas for your review. Write down notes.

Answer the Questions ● Use your notes to help you write answers to the three book review questions. Also make sure to state the title and the author of your book.

Writing the First Draft

Review Your Draft ● Have you answered the three questions? Are your sentences clear?

Revising and Editing

Check for Errors ● Make sure you have spelled the author's name correctly. Also remember to underline the book's title. After you have checked your review for errors, write a neat final copy to share.

TIP: The revising section in your handbook will help you make your review exciting and interesting to read. (See pages 43-47.)

Collection Chart

The questions in this chart will help you think about your book. There are separate ideas for fiction (made-up) and nonfiction (true) books.

 ## What is the book about?

Fiction: What happens to the main character? Where and when does the story take place?

Nonfiction: Is the book about a person, a place, an animal, or something that happened? Name one part of the book that seems important.

Why do I like this book?

Fiction: Does it have a lot of action?
Do you like the main character? Why?
Do you have a favorite part?

Nonfiction: Does the book contain interesting information?
Are the pictures colorful? Helpful?

What main idea did the author share?

Fiction: What did you learn in this book?

Nonfiction: Why do you think the author wrote this book? What did you learn?

Student MODEL

Here is Jennifer Sonshine's review of a fiction book. Each paragraph answers one of the review questions.

The *Summer I Shrank My Grandmother*

1 Have you ever thought about shrinking your grandmother? You can read about this crazy idea in The *Summer I Shrank My Grandmother* by Elvira Woodruff.

2 Wow! I want to read this book again. It was fun figuring out what the title really meant!

3 This book shows how you can use your imagination. Ms. Woodruff must know kids need good ideas to fill up summer vacation! Maybe I'll write a book next summer.

Hello, dear!

E L E M E N T S of Literature

The words listed below will help you understand and write reviews about stories and books.

An **autobiography** tells the true story of the writer's life.

A **biography** tells a true story about another person's life.

A **character** is a person in a story.

Dialogue is the talking between characters in a story.

The **ending**, or resolution, brings a story to a close.

An **event** is a specific action in a story.

Fiction is an invented or made-up story.

The **moral** is the lesson in a fable or tale.

A **myth** is a story created to explain a mystery of nature.

The **narrator** is the person or character who is telling the story.

Nonfiction is writing that is true.

The **plot** is the action in a story.

The **problem**, or conflict, in a story leads to all of the action.

The **setting** is the time and place of a story.

The **theme** is the main idea or message being written about.

Writing Business Letters

Writing business letters can help you in many ways. You can send for things you want, ask for information you need for a project, or even try to solve a problem.

What Makes a Letter a Business Letter?

A **business letter** is unlike a note or a letter you write to a friend. It is more serious, and it is about only one subject. Business letters look alike, too, because they follow the same form. This chapter will show you how to write these special letters.

Types of Business Letters

Two types of business letters are described on this page: *a letter asking for information* and *a letter to solve a problem.*

A Letter Asking for Information ● Let's say you need information for a science project. Or maybe you want to know how to join a fan club. You can write a letter of request asking for this information. Here's what you should include:

    ✳ **Explain why you are writing.**
    ✳ **Ask any questions you have.**
    ✳ **State what you would like.**
    ✳ **Thank them for their help.**

A Letter to Solve a Problem ● Let's say you have to wait outside too long before the school doors open. Or let's say you ordered special dog treats for old Mutt (your dog), and they sent you a book about dog tricks! You can write a letter to try to solve the problem. Here's how:

    ✳ **Describe the problem.**
    ✳ **Explain a possible cause of the problem.**
    ✳ **Suggest a way to solve the problem.**
    ✳ **Thank them for their help.**

Parts of a Business Letter

Below are the six parts of a business letter. The sample letter on the next page shows each part.

1 Heading: your address and the date.

2 Inside Address: the name and address of the person or company you are writing to. If the person has a special title, add a comma and the title after his or her name.
EXAMPLE: Mr. Lee Cheng, Life Scientist

3 Salutation: a way of saying hello. Always use a colon (:) after the person's name. Use *Mr.* for men and *Ms.* for women.
EXAMPLE: Dear Mr. Cheng:

4 Body: the main part of the letter. This is where you say what you want and give the important details.

5 Closing: a way of saying good-bye. Use *Sincerely, Very truly,* or *Yours truly.* Always place a comma after the closing.

6 Signature: your name under the closing. If you are using a computer, skip four lines and type your full name. Then sign your name between the closing and your typed name.

Student MODEL *Asking for Information*

Joey Jebrock sent a letter to a local expert, asking for information about the animal communities in the Bay Area.

1 68 Appleton Avenue
San Rafael, CA 94901
January 16, 1995

2 Mr. Lee Cheng, Life Scientist
U.S. Environmental Protection Agency
75 Hawthorne Street
San Francisco, CA 94105

Dear Mr. Cheng: **3**

Our third-grade class is studying communities. My group is studying animal communities in the Bay Area. Our teacher told us that your agency has been doing a lot of work with these communities.

4 Would you please send us information about the animals in and around the Bay Area. We would like to know how you do your work, too.

Also, please send us the titles of books you think are good about our topic. One or two titles would be fine.

Thank you.

Sincerely, **5**

6 Joey Jebrock
Joey Jebrock

Writing a Business Letter

Prewriting
Planning Your Writing

Know Your Purpose ● Decide if you are writing a letter to ask for information or to solve a problem.

Collect Ideas ● Plan what to say in your letter, using the information on page 123.

Writing the First Draft

State Your Ideas ● Explain what you want very clearly. (In the model letter, Joey explained that he wanted information about animal communities.)

* Follow the form for a business letter.

* Write short paragraphs, and use only one side of the paper.

Revising
Improving Your Writing

Review Your Ideas ● Make sure you have included all the important information in your letter.

Improve the Style ● Make sure your letter is easy to read. Rewrite parts that don't sound right to you.

Editing and Proofing

Check for Errors ● Check your writing for punctuation and spelling errors. Make sure you have spelled all names correctly.

Check the Form ● Review the form of your letter. (It should look pretty much like the model on page 125.) Then complete a neat copy of your letter to send.

TIP: On page 129, you can learn how to address an envelope and fold your letter.

Student MODEL *Solving a Problem*

The letter below is from a student who is trying to solve a problem.

1860 Ninth Avenue
Keystone, New York 12183
October 10, 1995

Mr. John Putney, Superintendent
Keystone School District
623 Madison Avenue
Keystone, New York 12183

Dear Mr. Putney:

I am in the third grade, and I am writing this letter to tell you about a problem. The kids on Bus 26 get to school so early that they have to stand outside until the doors open.

Describe the problem.

Bus 26 picks me up at 7:30. The bus leaves us off at school at 8:00. School doesn't start until 8:30, and the doors are locked until 8:20. It is cold in the morning. What will we do when it snows?

Explain the cause.

I think we should be able to wait in the library or the gym. Some kids like to read. Some kids like to play ball.

I hope you can solve this problem.

Give a solution.

Sincerely,

Janna Morris

Janna Morris

Sending Your Letter

Addressing the Envelope

- The post office prefers that you use all capital letters and no punctuation marks when you address an envelope. Also use the two-letter abbreviations for states. (See page 313 for a list of abbreviations.)

- Place your return address in the top-left corner of the envelope. Put the stamp in the top-right corner.

```
JANNA MORRIS
1860 NINTH AVE
KEYSTONE NY 12183



              MR. JOHN PUTNEY SUPERINTENDENT
              KEYSTONE SCHOOL DISTRICT
              623 MADISON AVE
              KEYSTONE NY  12183
```

Folding Your Letter

- Fold your letter into three equal parts.
- Crease the folds firmly.
- Put your letter into the envelope, and you're in business!

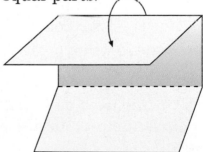

Writing to Explain

Explanations are everywhere—in science books, in cookbooks, in Lego sets, even on the back of cereal boxes (for contests). Some explanations help us understand things. Others are called "directions." They help us do something. Here's an example set of directions:

Test Your Flexibility

1. Stand up and put your feet together.
2. Bend slowly at the waist and try to touch the floor in front of your toes. Don't bend your knees . . . or bounce!
3. Stay in this position for about five seconds. (If you can do this, you have good flexibility.)

On the next few pages, we'll show you how to write helpful directions . . . so follow along!

Writing Directions

Prewriting
Planning Your Writing

Choose a Topic ● Think of something you like to do, or make, or some special place you like to go.

Select a Form ● Decide if your directions will be in list form or in a paragraph. (See the examples on pages 133-135.)

Writing the First Draft

Write Out the Steps ● List and number all the steps in your directions, or write your directions in a paragraph.

Choose the Best Words ● Use words that make your explanation clear.

* Actions words like *put, stand,* or *take* tell the reader what to do.
* Order or time words like *next, then,* or *after* help the reader follow each step.

Revising
Improving Your Writing

Read It Over ● Carefully review your directions. Use these questions to help review and revise your work.

* ✳ Is each step or sentence clear?
* ✳ Are your steps in the right order?
* ✳ Did you use exact words?

Editing and Proofing

Correct It ● Check your revised writing for errors in spelling and punctuation. Double-check any numbers or measurements. Then write a neat final copy to share.

Four Kinds of Directions

1 How to Make Something

Jenny explains how to make a butterfly hatchery. Study her action words—*punch*, *find*, *put*, *stand*, *replace*, *watch*, and *take*. These words tell the reader what to do.

Making a Butterfly Hatchery

Materials: one quart glass jar with lid, caterpillar, leaves, twig

1. **Punch** holes in the lid of a quart glass jar.
2. **Find** a caterpillar. Look on tomato plants, trees, or bushes.
3. **Put** the caterpillar in the jar. Also put leaves from the plant you found it on in the jar.
4. **Stand** a small twig up in the jar.
5. **Put** the lid on the jar. Put the jar in a shady place.
6. **Replace** the leaves in the jar every two days.
7. **Watch** every day. First the caterpillar stops eating. Then it spins a cocoon on the twig. Finally, the cocoon splits open and a butterfly comes out.
8. **Take** the lid off. Don't touch the butterfly. When its wings are ready, it will fly away.

2

How to Do Something

The author of this model, Joey, explains how to recycle jars and cans. He uses words like *first*, *next*, and *finally* to let readers know the order in which to do things. This explanation is written in paragraph form.

Recycling Jars and Cans

Recycling jars and cans is easy if you follow these steps. First, wash out all of your empties. Next, take the paper off them. Jar lids can't be recycled, so throw them into the trash. Then put the clean jars and cans into a clear plastic bag or in a recycling container. Finally, put them in the proper place to be picked up.

3

How to Get Someplace

In this model, Rachel explains how to get to her house from school. See how Rachel uses *building names*, *street names*, and *exact numbers*, and tells the reader whether to turn *right* or *left*.

How to Get to My House from School

1. After you walk out of the school's front door, turn left.
2. Walk two blocks. Turn right at the traffic light.
3. Walk three blocks to Moffitt's Market on the corner. Turn left. That's Hill Street.
4. Go down three houses. My house is on the right. My address is 3827 Hill. You should see our yellow door.

How to Have Some Fun

4

Writing crazy directions can be fun. Roberto's model explains how to work his homework machine.

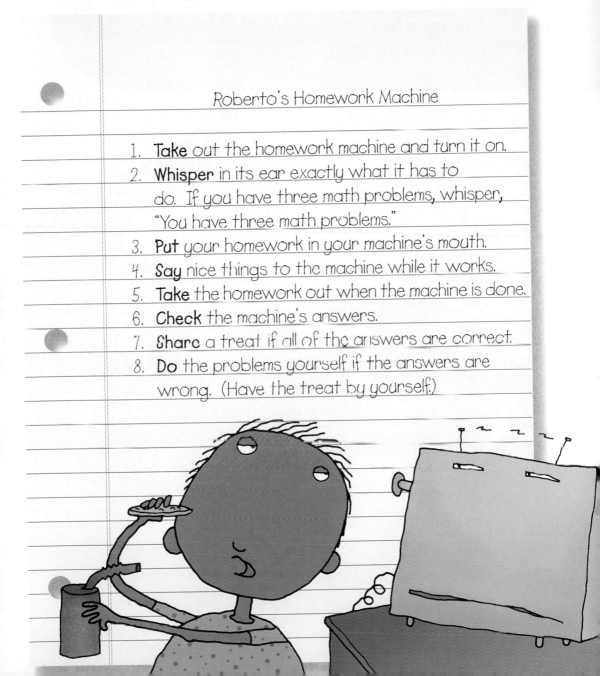

Roberto's Homework Machine

1. **Take** out the homework machine and turn it on.
2. **Whisper** in its ear exactly what it has to do. If you have three math problems, whisper, "You have three math problems."
3. **Put** your homework in your machine's mouth.
4. **Say** nice things to the machine while it works.
5. **Take** the homework out when the machine is done.
6. **Check** the machine's answers.
7. **Share** a treat if all of the answers are correct.
8. **Do** the problems yourself if the answers are wrong. (Have the treat by yourself.)

Research Writing

Using the Library

The **library** is your one-stop information place. It is loaded with facts, photos, and ideas on all sorts of topics. All of this information is found in magazines, newspapers, books, videos, CD's, and more. Libraries are sometimes called media centers because they contain so many different types of materials.

Finding Your Way

Your library is really helpful when you are working on reports and other big projects. This chapter explains how the materials in libraries are organized, and how you can find the information you need.

Using the Card Catalog

You can study lizards outdoors if you know where to find them. (Know any lizard trackers?) Or you can study lizards in the library. You'll need to use the **card catalog** to get started. It tells you which books are in your library. Each book usually has three cards in this catalog, and they are listed in ABC order.

1 **Title Cards:** There is a **title card** for every book in the library. If a title begins with *A, An,* or *The,* look up the next word.
The Yucky Reptile Alphabet Book

2 **Author Cards:** Every book has an **author card**. The last name of the author comes first on this card.
Smith, Trevor

3 **Subject Cards:** Many books are also listed on **subject cards**.
You can look under the subject heading LIZARDS or REPTILES to find books about lizards.

Steps to Follow ● Follow these steps when you use the card catalog:

* If you know the title of a book, look in the card catalog (or computer) for the title card.
* If you only know the author's name, look up the author card.
* If you only know that you need information about a subject, look up the subject card.

Example Catalog Cards

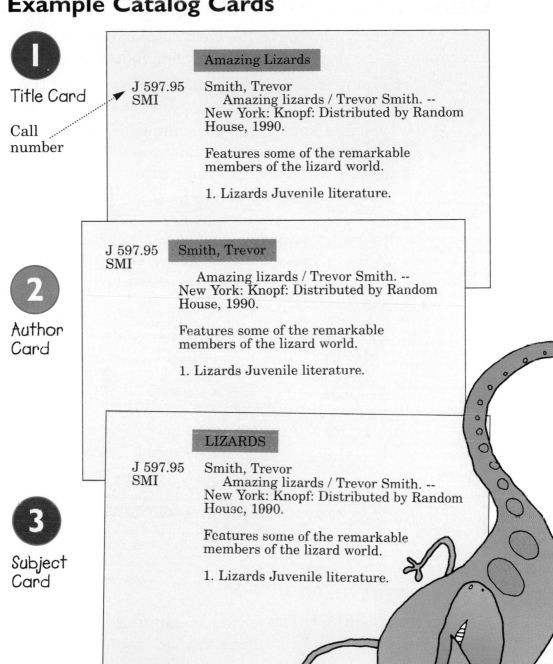

1.

Title Card

Call number

> **Amazing Lizards**
>
> J 597.95   Smith, Trevor
> SMI   Amazing lizards / Trevor Smith. --
> New York: Knopf: Distributed by Random
> House, 1990.
>
> Features some of the remarkable
> members of the lizard world.
>
> 1. Lizards Juvenile literature.

2

Author Card

> J 597.95   **Smith, Trevor**
> SMI
>   Amazing lizards / Trevor Smith. --
> New York: Knopf: Distributed by Random
> House, 1990.
>
> Features some of the remarkable
> members of the lizard world.
>
> 1. Lizards Juvenile literature.

3

Subject Card

> **LIZARDS**
>
> J 597.95   Smith, Trevor
> SMI   Amazing lizards / Trevor Smith. --
> New York: Knopf: Distributed by Random
> House, 1990.
>
> Features some of the remarkable
> members of the lizard world.
>
> 1. Lizards Juvenile literature.

Using a Computer Catalog

Your library may have the card catalog on computer. After reading the directions on the screen, follow these tips:

✻ Try typing in a title or an author, if you know this information.

✻ Or type in a keyword. For example, if you type *lizards,* the computer will show you a list of materials with *lizards* in their titles.

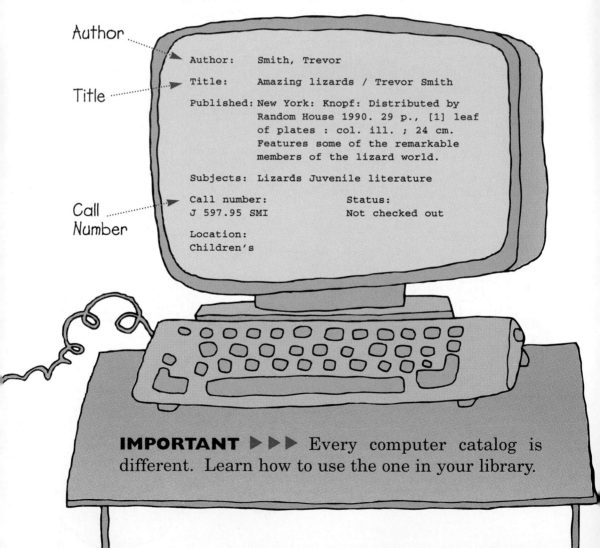

Author

Title

Call
Number

```
Author:    Smith, Trevor

Title:     Amazing lizards / Trevor Smith

Published: New York: Knopf: Distributed by
           Random House 1990. 29 p., [1] leaf
           of plates : col. ill. ; 24 cm.
           Features some of the remarkable
           members of the lizard world.

Subjects:  Lizards Juvenile literature

Call number:              Status:
J 597.95 SMI              Not checked out

Location:
Children's
```

IMPORTANT ▶ ▶ ▶ Every computer catalog is different. Learn how to use the one in your library.

How to Find a Book

Once you've found the card for a book, copy down the **call number**. The call number tells you where a book is located on the shelves. Now you are ready to find your book.

Finding Nonfiction ● Nonfiction (true) books are arranged on the shelves in number order. Here are some things you need to know:

* Some call numbers have one or more letters at the end. The book with the call number 973A comes before 973B on the shelf.

* Some call numbers have decimals, like 973.19 or 973.2. They may be a little harder to find. But you can ask the librarian for help.

Finding Fiction ● Fiction (made-up) books are on special shelves together. They are in ABC order by the author's last name. Sometimes fiction books have the first two letters of the author's last name on the spine, like CL for Beverly Cleary.

Finding Biographies ● Biographies have their own shelves, too. Biographies are true books about people. They are arranged by the last name of the person written about. Ask your librarian for help locating these special shelves.

Using an Encyclopedia

An **encyclopedia** is a set of books (or a CD) that has articles on every topic you can imagine. The topics are in ABC order, just like words in a dictionary. Each article gives you a lot of helpful information. You may also find a list of related topics at the end of each article. Look these up to find even more information!

 Your library may have several different sets of encyclopedias. You'll get to know your topic even better by using more than one encyclopedia.

Using Other Reference Books

Reference books give a lot of useful information. Encyclopedias are common reference books. Dictionaries and atlases are also reference books. They are kept in a special section of the library. Here are some other common reference books that your library may have:

The World Almanac and Book of Facts has facts and figures on sports, countries, languages, history, and many other topics.

Raintree Illustrated Science Encyclopedia covers science topics.

Something About the Author tells about writers and illustrators and gives their addresses.

Encyclopedia of Presidents has one book on each president.

From Sea to Shining Sea covers the 50 states, the District of Columbia, and Puerto Rico.

Understanding Parts of Books

Books are easier to use when you understand their parts:

- The **title page** is usually the first page with printing on it. It gives the title of the book, the author's name, the publisher's name, and the city where the book was published.

- The **copyright page** comes next. It gives the year the book was published. This can be important. An old book may have information that is no longer correct.

- The **table of contents** tells the names of the chapters and sections in the book and their page numbers.

- The **chapter and section headings** tell you what type of information will be covered in each part of a book.

- The **captions** give important information about pictures or illustrations. They are usually located below the pictures.

- The **glossary** explains special words used in the book. It's like a mini-dictionary. You will find the glossary near the back of a book.

- The **index** is an ABC list of all the topics in the book. It also gives the page number where each topic is covered. The index is in the back of the book.

Writing Classroom Reports

The world is full of things to care about: dolphins, spiders, volcanoes, tornadoes, space, holidays, peanuts. (Yes, peanuts. Just think what life would be like without peanut butter!) In a report, you get to share all kinds of neat information about a subject that is important to you.

Getting Started

Andy Levin liked and cared about hawks. He knew something about them from his dad. He found out even more when he wrote his report. This chapter will show you what he did to write a good classroom report. Then you can do the same.

Student  MODEL

Beginning

Middle

Ending

AMAZING HAWKS
by Andy Levin

I have liked hawks for a long time. An interesting thing about hawks is what they eat. If you knew what they ate, you would be glad that hawks aren't in charge of school lunches!

Hawks eat mice, snakes, and grasshoppers. A hawk kills a mouse by grabbing onto it with its claws and shaking it. Then the hawk pecks at it. My dad once saw a hawk eat a snake. He said, "The hawk chopped the snake in half and then gobbled up each half." Hawks eat grasshoppers whole. They need this food for energy.

Experts say hawks live a long time, but not longer than humans. Some live 10 to 15 years. Others live to be 30 years old.

Hawks have big wings and spend a lot of time flying. The World Book says that one kind of hawk has a wingspan of 44-47 inches. A hawk spreads its wings so it can get to its home in high cliffs. Another reason hawks have big wings is to help them dive at 350 miles per hour. This high speed helps them catch their prey.

Hawks are amazing! They are as graceful as high divers and as fast as some airplanes. My dad is glad I've learned more about hawks. So am I.

Prewriting
Planning Your Writing

Writing a Report

Select a Good Subject ● Choose a subject you care about.

* If you've been assigned a general subject like birds, make a list of your favorite ones.

* Look for more examples of your subject in an encyclopedia or textbook. Also ask your friends or family members for ideas.

* Think about each example on your list. Choose the best one for your report.

Write Questions About Your Subject ● Think of questions that can't be answered with a *yes* or *no*. Here's a good question: Why do hawks have such big wings?

Copy your questions on note cards or half sheets of paper. (One question per note card.) Or copy your questions on a gathering grid. (See page 148 for a model.)

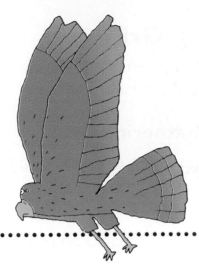

Learn About Your Subject ● Use at least two different sources. Andy learned about hawks from an encyclopedia, a book, and his dad.

Here is a list of sources for information:

**encyclopedias, books,
magazines, newspapers,
the Internet, filmstrips, videos,
CD's,** and **interviews.**

Answer Your Questions as You Read ● Write your answers on the note cards or gathering grid. When you find important information, write down only the main ideas. (This is called taking notes.)

If a book says . . .   Hawks capture living animals and kill them instantly for food.

You can write . . .   capture living animals
kill fast and eat

Gathering Grid

A gathering grid helps you organize the information you collect about your subject.

Tips for a Gathering Grid

- Use a big piece of paper so you have space to write answers.
- Draw lines to form a grid.
- Neatly fill in the grid as you go along.

Subject   Sources of Information

Hawks	Encyclopedia World Book	Book Hawks	Interview Dad
1. What does a hawk eat?	mice, rats, snakes	grasshoppers (whole)	snakes (tell story about Dad seeing one being eaten)
2. Why do hawks have such big wings?	to help them dive at 350 miles per hour; some wing-spans 44" - 47"	to make them fly fast to catch prey	so they can fly higher; so they can nest in cliffs
3. About how long does a hawk live?	some 30 years		10-15 years

Questions   Answers

Writing
the First
Draft

Write the Beginning ● Your first paragraph should tell what your report is about and hook the readers' interest. Andy uses humor to hook his readers:

> If you knew what they ate, you would be glad that hawks aren't in charge of school lunches!

Here are some other ways to hook readers:

* Start with a question:

    Did you know that hawks can dive at 350 miles an hour?

* Share an interesting story:

    My dad once saw a hawk eat a snake. . . .

Write the Middle ● Write the main part of your report. The answers to each of your questions belong together in the same paragraph. For example, all of Andy's information about what hawks eat is in his second paragraph.

Write the Ending ● Make your ending strong. Tell what you have learned or how you feel about your topic. Andy wrote his last paragraph in this way:

> Hawks are amazing! They are as graceful as high divers and as fast as some airplanes. My dad is glad I've learned more about hawks. So am I.

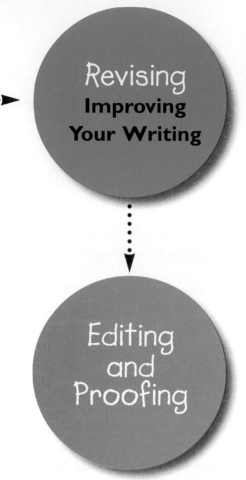

Revising
**Improving
Your Writing**

Editing
and
Proofing

Read and Review ● The questions listed below will help you review your first draft. (Also have a friend or classmate review your work.)

* Did you include a beginning, a middle, and an ending?

* Is each middle paragraph about one idea? (Does it answer one question?)

* Are there any parts that need more information or that sound unclear?

Check for Errors ● Check the spelling of all names and important terms. Make sure that all of your sentences begin with a capital letter and end with the correct punctuation mark.

Plan Your Final Copy ● Are you going to add pictures or charts to your report? Are you going to make a cover for it? Also check with your teacher. She may want you to write your final copy in a certain way.

Writing a Report Checklist

Prewriting

- [ ] Select a good subject.
- [ ] Write questions about your subject.
- [ ] Learn about your subject.
- [ ] Answer your questions on note cards or a gathering grid.

Writing the First Draft

- [ ] **Write the Beginning** • Introduce your subject.
- [ ] **Write the Middle** • Answer your questions.
- [ ] **Write the Ending** • End with an important idea about your subject.

Revising

- [ ] Read your first draft.
- [ ] Have someone else review it.
- [ ] Make changes.

Editing and Proofing

- [ ] Check for errors.
- [ ] Plan your final copy.

Writing Photo Essays

Have you ever opened a book with photos and said, "Cool!" We have, too. Photos can show you what words can only tell you. They make learning more real and exciting.

The "Show and Tell" of Writing

Photo essays share information or tell stories using words and photos. For example, in *Rosie, A Visiting Dog's Story,* by Stephanie Calmenson, the words tell how a dog cheers up sick children. The photos show Rosie at work in a hospital.

In this chapter, we'll show you part of a photo essay by students just like you. Then we'll tell you how to write your own.

Student MODEL

Beginning ● Three students named Paul Sanfiorenze, James Yan, and Shlomo Isakhrov created a photo essay about a resource teacher and her students. The title of their photo essay is "Helping Out: Mrs. Dulitz and Her Class." Here is the first page:

Introduction

Meet Mrs. Dulitz. She's a resource teacher. She teaches blind children and also students who have a hard time seeing.

She says she usually gets her students in kindergarten and watches them grow and mature through sixth grade.

Teachers all over the world are teaching children who are blind or almost blind. You can read about it in this book.

The pictures were taken by James, Shlomo, and Paul.

Middle ● The main part of the photo essay shows students using special equipment. Here is one page from this part of the essay:

Jenna Godino and Faith Washington are learning to tell time with a braille clock (on the left). The clock on the right is a plain play clock.

TIP: *Remember:* Photos can show you what words can only tell you. What does this photo show you?

Another Middle Page

Sarah Badillo is only in first grade,
and she knows how to use a braille
typewriter. She uses it in class.

Ending ● The photo essay ends with a look to the future.
(There is no photo on the last page.)

Years ago there wasn't as much technology to help the
blind as there is today. Today we have laser canes and braille
keyboards for computers.

Mrs. Dulitz and her class look forward to the future.
Maybe there will be even better gadgets for her students to use.

Prewriting
Planning Your Writing

Writing a Photo Essay

Select a Subject ● Make a list of different people with interesting jobs or hobbies. Choose one person for your photo essay.

Learn About Your Subject ● Write down what you know about your subject. Then ask this person some questions to find out more about his or her job or hobby.

Take the Photos ● Take 10 to 12 photos of your subject doing different things. You could show a rollerblader putting on the equipment, skating with friends, taking care of her skates, and so on.

Decide How to Use the Photos ● Get your pictures developed and put them in the best order for your essay.

Writing the First Draft

Tell Your Story ● Write sentences to go along with your photos.

* Introduce your subject on the beginning page of your essay.
* End your essay with an interesting idea about your subject.

Read and Review ● Look over your writing. Are all of your sentences clear? Do your words match with each picture? Did you include interesting details?

Revising
Improving Your Writing

Editing and Proofing

Check for Errors ● Check your work for spelling and punctuation errors. Then make a final copy of your essay in book form. (See page 33 for help.)

Writing Stories, Tales, and Plays

Writing Realistic
Stories

Realistic stories are true to life. In many ways, they are the opposite of fantasy stories. You can't have your main character put on baseball shoes and suddenly leap over the bleacher seats. (Nice idea, though!)

Starting Out

A realistic story should sound like it could have really happened. You can even use a real event as a starting point. Just make enough changes so it becomes made-up. Read the model and the guidelines on the next four pages to see how it is done. Then get started on your own story.

Student MODEL

Jonathan Rosenbaum's story is based on a personal event, but a lot of it is made-up. For example, he changed the names of the main characters, added some new details, and made the ending a little different.

A Very Far Hit

"Batter up!" called the umpire. Bill played on the Tigers, and his team was playing the Bees.

The Bees were up first. Bill thought, "I'm glad it's not me. Maybe I'll strike out."

The first batter was Nick, and he hit a fly ball. "Got it!" shouted Bill as he caught Nick's fly.

After three outs, the Tigers came to bat. It was Bill's turn to bat first. Back came that scary feeling. Bill didn't want to strike out. He just needed to remember the coach's tip about holding the bat and following through.

"Here it comes!" shouted the pitcher.

Bill stood ready. The ball headed straight toward the plate, and Bill whipped it with his bat. The hit sounded like metal garbage lids clanging. The ball flew deep into the outfield.

The coach whistled, "Wow, whee! What a hit!"

Later that evening, Bill got a phone call from his grandmother in Pittsburgh. She said, "Hi, Bill. A funny thing happened this afternoon. A baseball shot through the kitchen window and landed in my lap!"

Bill laughed. He knew his mom had been on the phone. "That was my ball, Grandma. Nice hit, hey?"

The main character

The problem

Exciting details

Clever ending

Prewriting
Planning Your Writing

Writing a Realistic Story

Choose a Topic ● You may already have a good idea for a story. If not, follow these steps:

* List at least six exciting, funny, or strange events that happened to you.

* Select the best event to use as the starting point for your story.

Test the Event ● If you can answer *yes* to these questions, your story idea is a winner!

* Can I remember a lot of details about this event?

* Will my classmates like to read about it?

* Can I think of ways to change it into a made-up story?

Your story should have some type of problem that needs to be solved. In the model story, Bill was afraid he was going to strike out.

Writing the First Draft

Choose a Way to Begin ● You can start by writing down what really happened in the event. Or you can jump right in to your made-up story.

Make Things Up ● Here are different ways to turn a real event into a made-up story. (Change at least two things.)

* Change the names of the characters.
* Change how the characters talk or act.
* Change where the action takes place.
* Change how the event begins or ends.
* Add more to the story.

Revising and Editing

Read and Review ● Read your story out loud. Change any parts that are hard to follow or sound uninteresting. (See the next page for ideas.)

Check for Errors ● Remember that your characters' words should be in quotation marks ("Batter up!" called the umpire). Also remember to start a new paragraph when someone new talks. After you check your story for errors, write a neat final copy to share.

Making Your Story Come Alive

Start Your Story Off with a Bang

Jonathan started his story in the middle of the action:

"Batter up!" called the umpire. Bill played on the Tigers, and his team was playing the Bees.

Have the Characters Think and Speak

Your story will seem more real if the characters think and speak.

Bill thought, "I'm glad it's not me. Maybe I'll strike out."
The coach whistled, "Wow, whee! What a hit!"

Use Action Words

Action words help readers hear and see the story.

"Here it comes!" shouted the pitcher.
Bill whipped it [the ball] with his bat.

Make Word Pictures

Have some fun with your words to make your story exciting.

The hit sounded like metal garbage lids clanging.

Writing Time-Travel
Fantasies

Would you like to see a dinosaur up close? Or ride in a spaceship? Or meet King Arthur and the Knights of the Round Table? Well, you can . . . when you write a **time-travel fantasy**!

What if . . .

Fantasies often begin with a question:

- What if I suddenly appeared in King Arthur's court on my skateboard?
- What if I found myself in a spaceship landing on a planet of robots?
- What if I crawled out of an old cardboard box and suddenly found myself nose to nose with a dinosaur?

To think like a fantasy writer, write a few wild questions of your own. Then read on to learn more about fantasy stories.

Thinking About Time Travel

Before you begin a time-travel fantasy, you should think about an interesting time and place to write about. This page will help you make your travel plans.

Choose a Time ● Where would you go if you could travel into the past or future? Would you travel back to the days of the gold rush, or way back to the days of the dinosaurs? Or would you travel into the future to a city on Mars? (See the time line on pages 382-391 for ideas.)

Learn About It ● If you choose a long-ago time, read and learn about it. Start with an encyclopedia or another book. Jenna found these facts for her story, "The Dinosaur Club." (See pages 168-169 for this story.)

> my favorite dinosaurs lived in Jurassic period
> (138-205 million years ago!)
>
> Brontosaurus—one of biggest dinosaurs
> - 80 feet long
> - small head, long neck
> - front legs shorter than back ones
> - ate plants

Decide How to Get There ● Now decide how to travel to this time. In a time machine? On a magical skateboard? In an old refrigerator box?

Prewriting
Planning Your Writing

Writing a Fantasy

Invent the Characters ● Pick one or two main characters to travel to the time and place you selected on the last page.

Find a Problem ● Choose a problem your characters face during their trip. Jenna made this web and then picked one problem for her story.

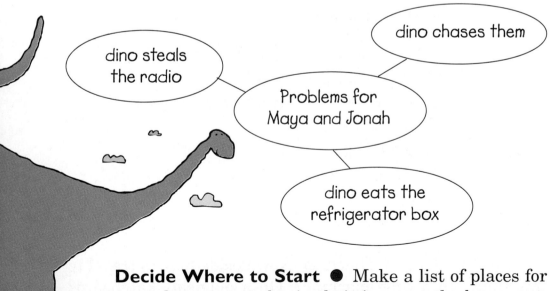

dino chases them

dino steals the radio

Problems for Maya and Jonah

dino eats the refrigerator box

Decide Where to Start ● Make a list of places for your characters to begin their journey: the basement, the garage, the parking lot, . . . Choose one.

Writing the First Draft

Take Off ● Create your fantasy story.

* Have your characters do and say things that tell who they are.
* Show how and where they travel.
* Use the facts you collected.

Include the Problem ● Show how your characters get into trouble. Then, later, show how they get out of it.

In Jenna's story, a brontosaurus takes a radio that belongs to Maya's brother. Maya tickles the dinosaur under its nose until it sneezes and sends the radio flying.

Revising Improving Your Writing

Review Your Draft ● Have you put in enough details to make your story interesting? Do your characters solve a problem? Make the changes you need.

Editing and Proofing

Check for Errors ● Look over your writing for spelling and punctuation errors. Then write a neat final copy to share.

Student MODEL

Here's a time-travel fantasy by Jenna Thompkins.

THE DINOSAUR CLUB

Maya walked into her backyard. She was carrying a portable radio she had borrowed from her brother's room. And she was dragging a big, empty refrigerator box.

"Cool!" said Maya's neighbor, Jonah, looking over the fence at the box. "We can make a fort!"

"It's going to be a clubhouse for my Dinosaur Club!" Maya said, thinking about the dinosaur book she had just read.

"What does the club do?"

"You'll see when you come inside," Maya replied, picking up the radio and crawling into the box. Jonah followed.

Suddenly the box began to spin and spin and spin. When it stopped, they tumbled out.

The main characters are introduced.

They travel in time.

An eighty-foot-long brontosaurus walked toward them. Its two front legs were shorter than its two back legs, but they were still huge.

A loud song suddenly blasted from the radio. The brontosaurus picked up the radio in its teeth and then sat down and fell asleep.

A problem occurs.

"It's taking a nap!" Maya said with amazement.

"Let's go home!" Jonah whispered.

Excitement builds.

"No way!" said Maya. "If I don't get that radio back, my brother will murder me!"

Maya thought hard and came up with an idea. She picked up a branch that had fallen off a tree and tickled the brontosaurus under its nose. The brontosaurus sneezed and sent the radio flying through the air. Maya caught it and scrambled into the refrigerator box, pulling Jonah behind her.

The problem is solved.

The minute they were inside the box, it began to spin and spin and spin. When they peeked out, Maya and Jonah were home.

"Want to go again tomorrow?" Maya asked. "I'll ask my brother, too!"

The characters return.

"Okay!" said Jonah. "But let's not bring his radio."

Writing
Plays

A **play** is a story that is acted out in front of an audience. People or animals in a play are called characters. They talk to each other and try to solve a problem. Plays can be fun to write because you get to tell the characters what to do and say.

Play Ideas

Ideas for plays are everywhere. You can write a play based on a real event or on a crazy idea you cook up. You can even write a play based on a well-known story. We'll help you turn a story into a play in this chapter. But first, let's see what a play looks like.

MODEL Play

This is the first scene for a play based on "The Three Little Pigs." (Longer plays are divided into scenes.)

··········Title

The Three Little Pigs

Characters: Pig 1, Pig 2, Pig 3, Wolf ◄·········· Cast

Setting

SCENE 1

Place: It is a beautiful spring day. The three pig brothers are in front of their houses. Pig 3 is putting the last bricks in a wall of his house. Pig 1 and Pig 2 are sitting in lawn chairs.

········· Dialogue

PIG 1: (with a laugh) Will you look at our goofy brother! He's still working on that brick mess of his. My beautiful straw house only took me a day to build.

PIG 2: Let's face it. He's always doing things the long, hard way. My wonderful stick house only took me two days to build.

Stage directions

PIG 3: (without sounding mad) Brothers, doing a job right is what counts, not how long it takes.

PIG 1: You're such a goody-goody.

PIG 3: Someday you'll thank me for building a strong house.

Prewriting
Planning Your Writing

Writing a Play

Choose a Story ● List some of your favorite tales and fables. Look through a book of well-known stories to jog your memory. Then circle one of the stories in your list to turn into a play. (Remember that long stories turn into long plays!) Here's a list one student made:

Favorite Tales and Fables

The Hare and the Tortoise

The Lion and the Mouse

The Three Little Pigs

Cinderella

Jack and the Beanstalk

It may be fun (and a little easier) to write a play with a partner.

List the Story Events ● Write down the most important events in your story. Here's an example from "The Three Little Pigs." (There are many ways to tell this story.)

STORY EVENTS
1. The three little pigs each build a house.
2. The wolf blows down the stick house.
3. He blows down the straw house.
4. Pigs 1 and 2 run to their brother's brick house.
5. The wolf tries to blow the brick house down.
6. The three little pigs catch him in a pot of hot water.

Plan the Scenes ● Divide the story events into scenes. A new scene means a new action is about to begin. (You can include more than one story event in a scene.)

SCENE 1
The three little pigs each build a house.

SCENE 2
The wolf shows up hungry. He blows down the stick house. Then he blows down the straw house.

SCENE 3
Pigs 1 and 2 run to their brother's brick house. Pig 3 lets his brothers in.

SCENE 4
The wolf tries to blow the brick house down but can't. The pigs catch him in a big pot of hot water as he comes down the chimney.

Writing the First Draft

Set the Stage ● Write down the setting for Scene 1. The setting tells where and when the action takes place. See the example setting on page 171.

Write the Dialogue ● Now write the scene by having your characters talk to one another. The dialogue has to tell the story. Your characters can talk any way you like.

You can make your play funny by adding some modern words and ideas. You can also add stage directions to describe the characters' actions.

EXAMPLE:

WOLF: I'll huff and I'll puff and I'll blow your house down!

PIG 3:   (with hands on hips) No way, you big fur ball! These walls are superglued!

When you finish Scene 1, move on to the next scenes. Keep going until you finish your play.

Revising
Improving Your Writing

Read and Review ● Use these questions as a guide when you read and review your play.

* Does each scene deal with an important part of the story?
* Do the characters' words and actions tell the story?
* Is my play easy to follow?

Share Your Script ● Ask friends or family members to read your play out loud. Listen for words or ideas that you would like to change.

Check for Errors ● Carefully check your play for spelling and punctuation errors. Then follow the form on page 171 when you write the final copy of your play.

Editing and Proofing

The best way to share a play is to act it out. That means actors must be selected. Lines must be learned. Costumes must be put together. Simple props must be made. And the popcorn must be popped! (Just kidding on the last point.)

Writing Poems

Writing Free-Verse
Poetry

Poetry is . . . what poetry does. Poetry sings. It dances. It laughs. It cries. Poetry is rainbow words and star bursts and whispers. Poetry is the richest part of language.

Wow! What does all of that mean? Well, poetry is like life. It can be about good times, sad times, and in-between times. A good-time poem will be full of rainbow words and star bursts. A sad-time poem may be all whispers.

The Poet in You

The good news is, everyone can write poems. This chapter will help *you* get started. You'll learn how to read and enjoy poems. And you'll learn how to write a free-verse poem. By the time you finish, you'll have all kinds of poems dancing in your head!

Making Friends with a Poem

Once you start writing poems, you will probably enjoy reading a lot of them, too. When you read poems, you learn how they look and sound. Follow these steps to make friends with each new poem you read.

 Read the poem to yourself two or three times.

 Read it out loud. (Listen to what it says.)

 Share the poem with a friend. (Talk about it.)

 Copy the poem in a special notebook.

Now make friends with this poem written by a student like you!

Elephant Poem

Rumbling
    Rumbling
Rumbling
12,000 pounds are coming.
Crashing,
bashing,
trashing,   mashing,
dashing,   gnashing,
on
        leaves.
Elephant noises all around.
                    —Claudia Mark

What Makes Poems So Special?

1 Poetry looks different. It's not hard to spot a poem. It won't take up much space on the page. And it may have a very interesting shape like this model poem:

No Homework
When my teacher says,
"No homework"—
my heart
feels like the sky on the Fourth of July
        firecrackers BANG!
        s*p*a*r*k*l*e*r*s sizzle
and
                                high
                            high
    fireworks shoot high
                —Kevin Liu

2 Poetry says things in special ways. In the model poem, Kevin makes a special comparison: *"my heart feels like the sky on the Fourth of July."* He also uses descriptive words that make the poem come alive: *BANG, s*p*a*r*k*l*e*r*s,* and *sizzle.*

3 Poetry sounds good. Read Kevin's poem out loud. Listen for the rhyming words: *sky, July,* and *high.* Also listen for consonant sounds that are repeated: *feels, Fourth,* and *firecrackers; sparklers* and *sizzle.* Rhyme and repeating sounds make poetry fun to hear.

Learning About Free Verse

There are many different kinds of poems. One kind is called **free-verse poetry**. A free-verse poem can be long or short. It can rhyme, but it doesn't have to. It can include special touches like s*p*a*r*k*l*e*r*s. You are *free* to write about your subject in any way you please.

"Elephant Poem" and "No Homework" on the last two pages are good examples of free-verse poetry. Another example is given below:

When I Grow Up

When I grow up, I would like to BE
      an artist who draws cartoons of cats
      a gymnast who wins the gold
      a ballerina who twirls on her toes
      a seamstress who makes quilts and clothes
      a photographer who takes pictures
        of daisies and roses
      a teacher who teaches grade three
      a writer who writes books for kids like ME

—Kristen Murphy

Kristen's poem looks a lot like a list. After the first line, she starts each new line in the same way: *"an artist who . . . ," "a gymnast who . . . ,"* and so on.

Prewriting
Planning
Your Writing

Writing Free Verse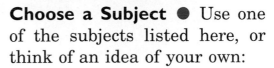

Choose a Subject ● Use one of the subjects listed here, or think of an idea of your own:

* ✳ jobs I'd like when I grow up
* ✳ what I wish for
* ✳ things that make me laugh
* ✳ ways to be a good friend
* ✳ good times

Collect Ideas ● Write your subject in the middle of a piece of paper. Circle the subject and map or cluster ideas around it. (See page 264 for a model map, or cluster.)

Writing the First Draft

List Your Ideas ● Study your cluster. Then list your best ideas. Also add new ideas that come to mind. (If your poem is about jobs, start your list like this: *When I grow up, I would like to BE . . .*)

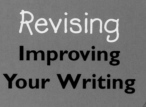

Revising
**Improving
Your Writing**

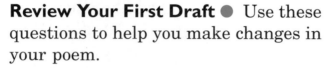

Review Your First Draft ● Use these questions to help you make changes in your poem.

* Do you like what your poem says? If not, rewrite unclear lines or add some new ideas.

* Do you like the way your poem looks? If not, think of another way to arrange your words.

* Do you like how your poem sounds? If not, maybe you need to add some rhyming words, or some words with repeating sounds.

Editing
and
Proofing

Correct Your Revised Poem ● Change or add punctuation marks and capital letters to make your poem clear. Check your spelling. Write a neat final copy.

Making Pleasing Sounds

Here are different ways poets make their poems pleasing to hear: (Use these ideas in your own poems, too!)

Rhyme ● Using rhyme is one way to make pleasing sounds in a poem:

> When I grow up, I would like to <u>be</u>
>   a writer who writes books for kids like <u>me</u>.

Repeating Sounds ● Repeating words can add special sound to a poem:

> The wind came <u>tapping</u>, <u>tapping</u>, <u>tapping</u>
> at my window.

Repeating consonant sounds helps, too:
> <u>S</u>ail <u>w</u>ith the <u>w</u>ind on a <u>s</u>imple <u>s</u>kiff.

Making Comparisons

Here are some of the special ways poets make comparisons in their poems.

✳ A **simile** makes a comparison using *like* or *as:*
> The race cars stayed together
>   like a school of fish.

✳ A **metaphor** makes a comparison without using *like* or *as:*
> Poetry is rainbow words and star bursts.

✳ **Personification** makes a thing seem like a person:
> The shadow crept closer and closer.

Writing Other Forms of Poetry

The fruit section in a grocery store is full of wonderful choices. There are big red apples and small purple plums; plump green grapes and bright yellow bananas. There are little, furry kiwi fruit (yuck!) and giant, striped watermelons. It's fun to try different fruits . . . except when they're furry!

Different Tastes, Different Forms

It's also fun to try different forms of poetry. This chapter talks about popular **traditional** and **invented forms**. You'll learn about nature poems and silly poems and poems with different shapes. Fruit is good for you; it helps build strong bodies. Poetry is good for you, too; it helps build strong hearts and minds. So start eating!

TRADITIONAL Poetry

Cinquain ● A cinquain (*say* `siŋ-kān) poem is fives lines long. To write a cinquain poem, follow the form listed below.

One-word title	Sneakers
Two describing words	Bouncy, fast
Three action words.	Walking, running, jumping
Four feeling words	Friends to my feet
One synonym for title	Shoes

Limerick ● A **limerick** is also five lines long. Lines one, two, and five rhyme; and lines three and four rhyme. A limerick is always about a silly subject.

> There once was a boy from Zion
> Who one day met up with a lion.
>   He pulled on its mane
>   And gave it a pain.
> But guess who ended up cryin'?

Haiku ● A **haiku** (*say* `hī-kü) poem is three lines long. The first and third lines have five syllables. The second line has seven syllables. The subject of a haiku poem is usually something in nature.

> See the red berries,
> fallen like little footprints
> on the garden snow.   —Shiki

Writing a Haiku Poem

Prewriting
Planning
Your Writing

Writing the First Draft

Collect Writing Ideas ● Go outside and make a list of the things you see. You may see a blossoming tree, a busy insect, a sleeping cat, and so on.

Select a Subject ● Was there one sight you found really surprising or colorful or interesting? Select that idea for your poem.

Write Three Lines ● Describe what you saw in the first two lines. In the third line, say something about your subject. Here's a first draft by student Blake Kosley:

> My rabbit lives in a wire cage.
> He jumps all over the place.
> He's hard for me to catch.

Count the Syllables ● Count the number of syllables in each line of your poem. Then add, take out, or move words to fit the haiku pattern:

Line 1: 5 syllables
Line 2: 7 syllables
Line 3: 5 syllables

Revising
Improving Your Writing

Check the Details ● Make sure that you have used the best words to describe your subject. (In Blake's poem about his rabbit, he saw that "hops" would be a better word than "jumps.")

TIP: Your haiku poem does not have to state complete sentences.

Editing and Proofing

Check for Errors ● Correct any spelling, capitalization, or punctuation errors. Then make a neat final copy of your poem. Here is Blake's finished poem:

Rabbit in a cage
hops all over the wire place
hard for me to catch!

INVENTED Poetry

Alphabet Poem ● An **alphabet** poem uses part of the alphabet to create a funny list poem.

Carefree
Dolphins
Even
Flip
Gracefully

Concrete Poem ● A **concrete** poem has a special shape or design.

Dizzy leaves slowly fall to the ground.

Five-W's Poem ● A **Five-W's** poem is five lines long. Each line answers one of the 5 W's (*who? what? where? when?* and *why?*).

My dog
curls up
on my bed
every night
because I let him.

Writing a Five-W's Poem

Prewriting
Planning Your Writing

Select a "Who" ● Make a list of silly and serious "who" ideas. Select one for your subject.

Make a 5-W's Chart ● Use a chart like this one to list ideas for your poem.

who?	what?	when?	where?	why?

Writing the First Draft

Make Your Poem ● Use the words in your chart to write your first draft. Use a separate line for each answer to a "W" question.

Revising and Editing

Check the Facts ● Make sure that you have answered all of the 5 W's.

Check Your Words ● Make sure that you have used the best words in your poem. For example, "My dog curls up" is better than "My dog sleeps."

Check for Errors ● Correct the mistakes and make a neat final copy to share.

3 The Tools of Learning

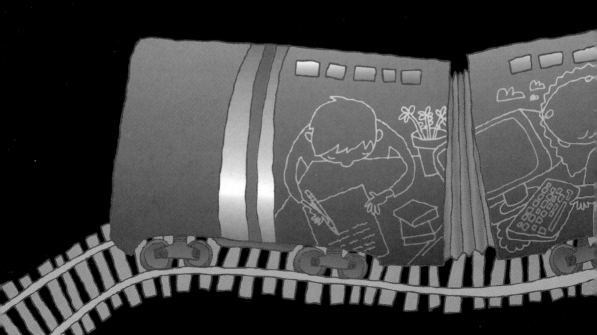

Improving Your Reading

Reading Graphics

You find **graphics** in many different places. They are on signs in your community, in directions to make things, and in the books and magazines you read. It is very important that you know how to "read" graphics because they help you learn.

Look at this!

This chapter tells you how to read three different kinds of graphics: symbols, diagrams, and tables. As you learn about these graphics, you'll be surprised at how much information they can give. *Remember:* Understanding graphics is like reading . . . without all the words.

Learning About Symbols

A **symbol** is a simple graphic, or drawing, that stands for something. Symbols can be divided into two groups.

● Some symbols stand for ideas or feelings.

a.    b.    c.

● Some symbols tell you what to do, or what not to do.

d.    e.    f.

Tips for Understanding Symbols

✳ Look at the graphic and think.
✳ Decide what it means.

Figure out what each symbol on this page means. (Check your answers below.)

a. Happiness, b. Love, c. Power, d. No Smoking, e. Telephone, f. Railroad Crossing

Learning About Diagrams

A **diagram** is a graphic that shows the parts of something. It may also show how something works.

Tips for Understanding Diagrams

* Look carefully at the graphic.
* Read the labels.
* Notice any pointer lines or arrows.

TWO EXAMPLES:

How You Get Electricity

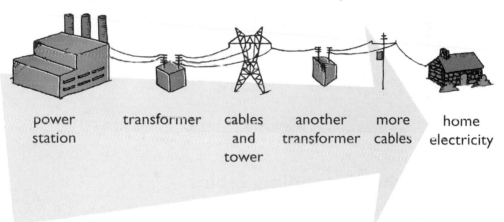

| power station | transformer | cables and tower | another transformer | more cables | home electricity |

Life Cycle of a Butterfly

Egg   Caterpillar   Pupa   Adult Butterfly

Learning About Tables

A **table** is a graphic that organizes words and numbers to help you find information quickly. Every table has two basic parts: rows go across, and columns go down. Here's an example:

Fourth Graders and Their Pets

Kind of Pet	Number of Kids
Dog	15
Cat	12
Fish	5
Bird	2
Hamster	2
Snake	1

Tips for Understanding Tables

* Read the title to see what the table is about.
* Look at the column headings. ("Kind of Pet" and "Number of Kids" are column headings.)
* Read across each row.
* Ask questions. For example, what does the table above tell you? How many kids have cats? How many kids have hamsters? (Ask some questions yourself.)

All Kinds of Tables

Here are some kinds of information you'll find in tables:

- Bus schedules (See the table below.)
- Class schedules
- TV schedules
- Lunchroom menus
- How much things cost

BUS DEPARTS FOR SPRINGFIELD

	8:00 a.m.	Noon	6:00 p.m.
Monday-Friday	🚌	🚌	🚌
Saturday	🚌	🚌	
Sunday		🚌	
Holidays	🚌	🚌	

(The little symbols tell you that a bus leaves at that time, on that day.)

Answer the following questions about the bus schedule:

  a. How many buses are leaving on Thanksgiving?
  b. Can you take a bus after 4 p.m. on Saturday?
  (Check your answers below.)

Reminders for Reading Graphics

* Read the title.
* Look at symbols, diagrams, and tables carefully.
* Read labels and notice pointers and arrows.
* Ask questions and think.

a. Two, b. No

Using Strategies to Read New Words

When you see a word you can't read, use the following **reading strategies** to help you.

1. Read and check.

First, look at the letters and letter patterns from left to right. Next, say the sound each letter or letter pattern represents. Then blend the sounds into a word you recognize.

* Look for consonant blends, such as "str" in *string.* Say the blend and then add the remaining sounds to it.

* Use what you know about vowel pairs, such as the "ai" in *paid,* to find letter patterns.

* Watch for r-controlled letter-sound patterns, such as "ir" in *first* or "air" in *pair.*

* Check to make sure the word you have said makes sense. If it doesn't make sense, think about the other words in the sentences. Then, use meaning and the sounds you do know and try again.

2. Look for word parts you know.

Longer words often have little words or word parts in them. For example, if you can read the little word *end*, you can probably read the words *bend*, *mend*, *send*, *blend*, and *ending*.

If you can read the word part *eed*, you can probably read the words *deed*, *seed*, and *speed*.

3. Apply what you know about syllables.

Vowel/Consonant, Vowel—as in su/per

Vowel, Consonant/Vowel—as in sev/en

Vowel, Consonant/Consonant, Vowel—as in sup/per

4. Look for prefixes, suffixes, and roots.

Longer words may be made up of smaller parts that you know. *Examples:*

	prefix		root		suffix
lioness =			lion	+	ess
monorail =	mono	+	rail		
unhealthy =	un	+	health	+	y

(See pages 214-223 in your handbook for the meanings of common prefixes, suffixes, and roots.)

5. Look for compound words.

Many big words are made up of two smaller words. We call these compound words. Here are a few examples: *sidewalk*, *farmyard* and *basketball*.

WHEW-EW-EW-EW-EW-EW

Reading
to Understand

Being a good reader means understanding what you read. And understanding is what reading is all about. It makes reading enjoyable and meaningful. It helps you learn and remember. If you can read and understand, you can discover wonderful things about your world.

Four Ways to Improve Your Reading:

1. Read often. (The more you read, the easier reading gets.)
2. Read a lot of different things. (Read stories, information books, newspapers, and magazines.)
3. Change your speed as you read. (For example, slow down when there are a lot of facts in the reading.)
4. Use reading strategies to help you understand better. (This chapter will show you how.)

Before, During, and After

A **reading strategy** is a plan to help you with your reading. Here are some strategies to help you read chapters in information books.

Before Reading

Preview: Study the title, the headings, the drawings, and so on.

Think About the Topic: Decide what you already know about the topic. And guess what the chapter will say.

Set a Purpose: Decide what you want to find out.

During Reading

Stop Along the Way: Think about each new idea as you read.

Look for Answers: Look closely at parts that answer questions you have about the topic.

Take Notes: Write down a few facts.

After Reading

Review: Did the reading answer your main questions? What new things did you learn?

Share: Talk about your reading with a classmate or a parent. Or write about it in your journal.

Know Want Learn

KWL is another good reading strategy. To use this strategy, you will need to make a KWL chart. Here's how to set up your chart:

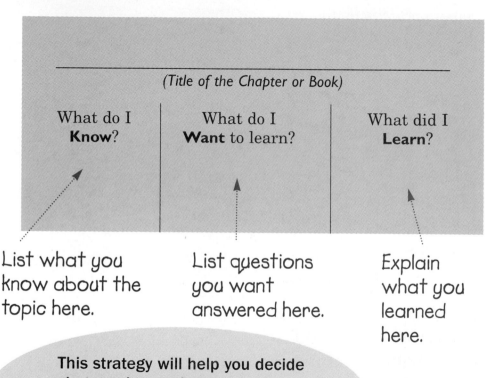

_____

(Title of the Chapter or Book)

| What do I **Know**? | What do I **Want** to learn? | What did I **Learn**? |

List what you know about the topic here.

List questions you want answered here.

Explain what you learned here.

This strategy will help you decide what you know about a topic for a classroom report . . . and what new things you may want to learn.

M O D E L KWL Chart

Here's how a completed KWL chart looks.

Building Machines and What They Do

K What do I know?	W What do I want to learn?	L What did I learn?
1. Building machines dig holes. 2. Some lift materials very high up. 3. Some stir cement.	1. What are the names of all the machines? 2. What are some new machines? 3. How is a building made?	1. Names I learned: tower, concrete mixer, crusher, excavator. 2. There are lots of pipes underground when a building is made. 3. There are . . .

Review your last column after the reading to see if you answered your questions. Maybe you'll want to add a few more questions to the **W** column, and read more about the topic.

Mapping

Mapping is a reading strategy that helps you organize ideas about a topic. All you have to do is write the topic in the middle of a sheet of paper. Then, as you read, draw a map of the main ideas and details about the subject. Here's how it's done:

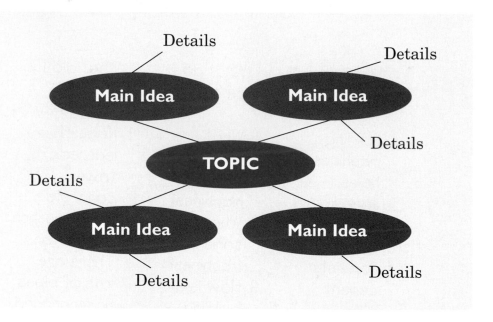

Finding the Main Ideas ● A *main idea* is an important part of your topic. You can find main ideas in headings, in bold print, or in the first and last sentences of paragraphs. Circle and connect these ideas to the topic.

Finding Details ● The *details* help explain each main idea. You can find details in the middle of paragraphs and in charts. Connect the details to the main idea.

MODEL Map

Here is how a reading map should look when it is completed.

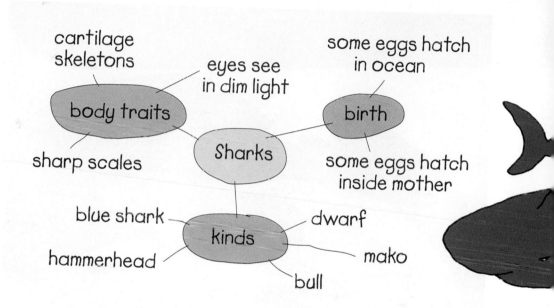

Writing to Learn

Here are two writing strategies that will help you understand what you read.

Stop 'n' Write ● Stop and write down your thoughts about ideas that seem important or surprising. Write a sentence or two and then get back to your reading.

Retelling ● Pretend you are telling a friend all about your reading. Write down everything he or she needs to know to understand the topic.

Improving Vocabulary and Spelling

Building Vocabulary
Skills

You see and hear new words just about every day. Your teacher might use a word you've never heard before. You might see a new word in a book. Once in a while, you might hear a new word on TV.

What's New?

A great sandwich takes a lot of fixin's. But a great vocabulary takes only one thing—learning new words. When you know a lot of words, it's easier to say exactly what you want to say. This chapter tells you how to build your vocabulary.

MUSTARD

KETCH

Learning New Words

1. Read, read, read!

The best way to learn new words is to read a lot. Books, magazines, and newspapers—read anything and everything!

2. Check nearby words.

The words that come before and after a new word may help you find its meaning. Check out the following sentence:

The animal expert talked about herons, cranes, and ibises

Ibises? That's probably a new word for you! But look at the words that come before it. Herons and cranes are both long-legged birds. So ibises are probably long-legged birds, too.

Here's another sentence with a new word:

At work, my mom uses a microscope to look at germs.

A microscope is an instrument for looking at very small things. What words in this sentence help you know that?

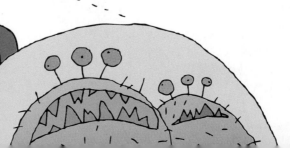

3. Keep a new-word notebook.

Make a special notebook for new words. Write the meaning and a sentence for each new word.

Vocabulary

Word	Meaning	Sentence
ibis	long-legged wading bird	The ibis is a wading bird with a long, curved bill.
microscope	an instrument used to see very small objects	Carla's mom uses a microscope to study water pollution.

4. Practice using new words.

Try using new words in your writing and speaking. For example, each week you could choose one new word from your notebook. Then you could think of ways to use it when talking to your friends and family. Using the word will help you remember it.

5. Look up the word in a dictionary.

Use a **dictionary** to look up new words. The dictionary gives you the meanings for each word plus much more.

Guide Words ● These are the words at the top of the page. They tell you where you are according to the alphabet.

Spelling ● The dictionary shows you the correct spelling for a word. It also shows if a word should be capitalized.

Pronunciation ● A dictionary shows you how a word is divided into syllables and how the word is said or pronounced. The pronunciation is given in parentheses ( ). The pronunciation key at the bottom of the dictionary page will help you, too.

How the Word Is Used ● The dictionary tells you if a word is a *noun,* a *verb,* an *adjective,* and so on.

Word History ● Some words have stories about their history—where they came from and their early meaning.

Synonyms ● For some words, the dictionary lists other words that mean the same thing.

Meaning ● Some words have only one meaning. Some words have many meanings.

Sample Dictionary Page

Guide Word —————— **sail**

¹sail \ 'sāl \ *n* **1:** a sheet of fabric (as canvas) used to catch enough wind to move boats through the water or over ice   **2:** the sails of a ship   **3:** a sailing ship   **4:** a voyage or trip on a sailing ship

¹sail 1

How the —————— **²sail** *vb* **1:** to travel on a boat moved by the wind   **2:** to travel by water
Word Is Used   **3:** to move or pass over by ship   **4:** to manage or direct the motion of (a boat or ship moved by the wind)   **5:** to move or glide along ‹the paper *sailed* through the air›

Meaning —————— **sail•boat** \ 'sāl-,bōt \ *n* **:** a boat that is equipped with sails

sail•fish \ 'sāl-,fish \ *n* **:** a fish related to the swordfish but with a large saillike fin on its back

sail•or \ 'sā-lər \ *n* **:** a person who sails

saint \ 'sānt \ *n* **1:** a good and holy person and especially one who is declared to be worthy of special honor   **2:** a person who is very good especially about helping others

Spelling —————— **Saint Ber•nard** \ 'sānt-bər-'närd \ *n* **:** a very large powerful dog bred originally in the Swiss Alps

saint•ly \ 'sānt-lē \ *adj* **:** like a saint or like that of a saint ‹a generous and *saintly* person › ‹a *saintly* smile › — **saint•li•ness** *n*

Synonym —————— **sake** \ 'sāk \ *n* **1:** ¹PURPOSE ‹for the *sake* of argument›   **2:** WELFARE, BENEFIT ‹for the *sake* of the country›

sal•able *or* **sale•able** \ 'sā-lə-bol \ *adj* **:** good enough to sell **:** likely to be bought

Pronunciation —————— **sal•ad** \ 'sal-əd \ *n* **1:** a dish of raw usually mixed vegetables served with a dressing   **2:** a cold dish of meat, shellfish, fruit, or vegetables served with a dressing

sal•a•ry \ 'sal-ə-rē, 'sal-rē\ *n, pl* **sal•a•ries** **:** a fixed amount of money paid at regular times for work done

Word History —————— **Word History** In ancient times, salt was used not only to make food taste better but to keep it from spoiling. Because salt was not always easy to get, Roman soldiers were given money to buy salt. The Latin word for salt money came to be used for any money paid to soldiers. Later the same word was used for money paid to public officials. The English word *salary* comes from this Latin word.

Pronunciation ——————
Key

\ ə \ abut	\ aú \ **out**	\ i \ tip	\ ò \ saw	\ ú \ foot
\ ər \ further	\ ch \ **chin**	\ ī \ life	\ òi \ coin	\ y \ yet
\ a \ mat	\ e \ pet	\ j \ job	\ th \ thin	\ yü \ few
\ ā \ take	\ ē \ easy	\ ng \ sing	\ th \ this	\ yu̇ \ cure
\ ä \ cot, cart	\ g \ go	\ ō \ bone	\ ü \ food	\ zh \ vision

6. Use a thesaurus.

A **thesaurus** is a book of words and their synonyms. Synonyms are words that mean almost the same thing. For example, if you look up *walk* in a thesaurus, you may find *stroll, hike,* and *step.* A thesaurus may also list antonyms for some words. Antonyms are words that mean the opposite.

Look for the Right Word ● Let's say you use a thesaurus to find just the right word for *hit* in the following sentence:

Josie _____ a hard liner up the middle.

Look up the word *hit* as you would in a dictionary. As you can see below, it is located between *history* and *hitch.*

Entry words   Synonyms

history   record, chronicle, annal

hit   strike, blow, knock, punch, smack, swat

hitch   fasten, hook, clasp, tie   *separate*

Antonym

Choose the Right Word ● Review the list of synonyms and choose the word that works best for your sentence. In the example, the best word seems to be *smack:*

Josie smacked a hard liner up the middle.

1. Divide the word into parts.

You can figure out the meaning of new words by learning about the three word parts:

 A **root** is a common word base.

 A **prefix** comes before the root and changes its meaning.

 A **suffix** comes after the root and changes its meaning.

Here's an example:

Root: cycl
(meaning *wheel*)

Preflx: unicycle   **Suffix:** cyclist

Prefix and Suffix: unicyclist

A Closer Look

Knowing the meaning of "uni" and "ist" helps you figure out the new words made from *cycl*. Let's see how:

* If you know that the prefix "uni" means "one," then *unicycle* must mean a cycle with one wheel.

* Then, if you know that the suffix "ist" means "someone who does something," then a *cyclist* must be somecne who rides a cycle.

* And a *unicyclist* must be someone who rides a cycle with one wheel.

Dictionary
of Prefixes, Suffixes, and Roots

It sure would be nice to have a 3-D Super Deluxe Wordmaster Machine. By pulling a few levers, you could make all kinds of new words. And by pushing a few buttons, you could find out what they mean. Sorry, we don't have a machine like this.

The Next Best Thing

But on the next nine pages, we do have a dictionary of common prefixes, suffixes, and roots. This special dictionary will help you build new words into your vocabulary. Since there are no levers to pull or buttons to push, we suggest that you work with your new words in a vocabulary notebook. (See page 209.)

Remember these things:
* A **root** is a word base (graph).
* A **prefix** comes before a root (<u>auto</u>graph).
* A **suffix** comes after a root (autograph<u>ed</u>).

Prefixes

Prefixes are word parts that come at the beginning of a word, before the root. They often change the meaning of the root.

amphi (both)

amphibian (an animal that lives both on land and in water)

anti (against)

antibody (part of the blood that works against germs)

astro (star, space)

astronaut (space traveler)
astronomy (study of the stars and outer space)

auto (self)

automatic (working by itself)

bi (two)

bicycle (two-wheeled vehicle)

cent (hundred)

century (100 years)

ex (out)

exit (to go out)

hemi, semi (half)

hemisphere (half of a sphere)
semicircle (half of a circle)

Prefixes

micro (very small)

microscope (tool for looking at very small things)

mono (one; *also see* uni)

monorail (train that runs on one track)

non (no, not; *also see* un)

nonfiction (not fiction or not true)

oct (eight)

octopus (a sea animal with eight armlike tentacles)

pre (before)

predict (to tell about something before it happens)

quad (four)

quadruped (an animal having four feet)

sub (under)

submarine (an underwater ship)

tri (three)

triangle (shape with three sides)

un (not; *also see* non)

unhealthy (not healthy)

uni (one; *also see* mono)

unique (one of a kind)

Suffixes

Suffixes are word parts that come at the end of a word, after the root. They often change the meaning of the root.

ed (past tense)

learned (to learn something in the past)

er (a person who)

baker (a person who bakes)

er (more)

tougher (more tough)

ess (female)

lioness (a female lion)

est (most)

fastest (most fast)

ful (full)

helpful (full of help)

ing (doing something)

talking (doing what it is to talk)

ist (a person who)

pianist (a person who plays piano)

less (without)

careless (without care)

Suffixes

ly (in some manner)

completely (in a complete manner)

ology (study of)

biology (study of living things)

s, es (plural, more than one)

trees (more than one tree)

y (having)

rosy (having a rose color)

Roots

A **root** is the main part of a word. It helps you understand the word's meaning. The next five pages list some common roots.

agri (field)

agriculture (growing things in fields; farming)

anni, annu (year)

anniversary (the same date on which an event happened)
annual (yearly)

aud (hear)

auditorium (a place to hear something)

biblio (book)

bibliography (list of books)

bio (life)

biography (writing about a person's life)

chron (time)

chronological (the time order in which things happened)

cycl, cyclo (wheel, circular)

bicycle (a vehicle with two wheels)
cyclone (a circular wind)

dem (people)

democracy (government by the people)

Roots

dent, dont (tooth)

denture (false teeth)
orthodontist (a person who straightens teeth)

derm (skin)

dermatology (the study of skin)

dynam (power)

dynamite (powerful explosive)

equi (equal)

equinox (day and night of equal length)

flex (bend)

flexible (able to bend)

geo (earth)

geography (study of the earth)

gram (letter, writing)

telegram (a letter sent from far away)
grammar (rules for writing)

graph (write)

autograph (to write one's own name)

hab, habit (live)

inhabit (to live in)

hydr (water)

hydrant (a place where firefighters get water to fight fires)

leg (law)

legal (related to the law)

log, ology (word, study)

prologue (words that come before the main part of a book)
zoology (study of animals)

magn (great; *also see mega*)

magnify (to make something appear larger)

man (hand)

manicure (to groom the hands)

mar (sea)

marine (related to the sea)

max (greatest)

maximum (the greatest amount possible)

mega (great, huge; *also see magn*)

megaphone (instrument that makes a sound louder)

mem (remember)

memo (a note to remember something)

meter (measure)

thermometer (an instrument that measures heat)

Roots

migr (move)

migrant (one who moves to find work)

min (small, less)

minimum (the smallest amount possible)
minus (less)

multi (many)

multicultural (including many cultures)

narr (tell)

narrative (writing that tells a story)

neg (no)

negative (meaning or saying no)

ped (foot; *also see* pod)

pedal (an instrument that is operated with the foot)

phon (sound)

telephone (a way sound travels)

photo (light)

photograph (a picture formed by light)

pod (foot; *also see* ped)

tripod (an object with three feet or legs)

port (carry)

portable (able to be carried)

scope (see)

otoscope (an instrument used for seeing inside the ear)

scribe (write)

inscribe (to write or carve letters onto something)

spec (look)

inspect (to look at carefully)

sphere (ball)

spherical (having the shape of a ball)

sum (highest)

summit (the highest point, top)

tele (far)

telescope (an instrument for seeing things that are far away)

therm (heat)

thermal (related to heat)

tox (poison)

toxic (poisonous)

vid (see)

video (the part of an electronic program that can be seen)
supervise (to oversee, or to look over)

zo (animal)

zoology (the study of animals)

Becoming a Better
Speller

Do you realize that when you can spell one word, you have a head start on learning to spell many others? That's right. For example, if you can spell *night*, you'll find it easier to spell *nights*, *nightly*, *nightfall*, and *nightstand*.

Basic Steps

There are spelling rules to help you, too. (The tricky part is that some words don't fit the rules. Yikes!) In this chapter we will tell you five ways to become a better speller:

* **Make a spelling dictionary.**

* **Use your senses to help you remember spellings.**

* **Use sayings and acrostics to help you remember spellings.**

* **Learn to proofread for spelling.**

* **Learn some basic spelling rules.**

1. Make a spelling dictionary.

In a small notebook, put one letter of the alphabet at the top of each page. (**A** goes at the top of the first page, **B** goes at the top of the second page, and so on.) Each time you learn a new word, write it in your spelling dictionary.

Next to each new word, write as many word relatives as you can think of. For example, *nights*, *nightly*, *nightmare*, *nightfall*, and *nightstand* are word relatives for *night*.

> Study the words in your spelling dictionary at least once a week. Soon you'll be able to spell the words without looking them up.

2. Use your senses.

Your senses, especially seeing and hearing, can help you become a better speller:

* Look at the word and say it.
* Cover it and try to "see" it in your mind.
* Write it from memory.
* Check the spelling.
* If the word is misspelled, try again.

3. Use sayings and acrostics.

A **saying** is a sentence that helps you remember how to spell a word. Here are two examples:

* **A friEND sticks with you to the END.** (This saying helps you remember that the **e** goes after the **i** in the word *friend*.)

* **People say BRrrr in FeBRuary.** (This saying helps you remember the "extra" **r** in *February*.)

An **acrostic** is a special kind of sentence. Each letter of the word you want to remember begins a word in a sentence.

Arithmetic:
A rat in the house might eat the ice cream.

Try this: Say the acrostic for *arithmetic.* As you say it, write down the first letter of each word. You've spelled the word! Arithmetic!

4. Proofread for spelling.

Proofreading for spelling is one of the last things you do before you call your writing finished. When you're not sure of a spelling, circle the word. Then check the spelling in a dictionary or in your handbook. (See pages 314-317 for a spelling list.)

5. Learn some basic spelling rules.

Rules can help you spell many words. But remember that there are **exceptions** to the rules. An exception is a word that doesn't fit the rule.

Words Ending in Y ● When you write the plurals of words that end in **y**, change the **y** to **i** and add **es**. Exception: If the word ends in **ey**, just add **s**.

puppy changes to **puppies**	**turkey** changes to **turkeys**
pony changes to **ponies**	**donkey** changes to **donkeys**

Consonant Ending ● When a one-syllable word with a short vowel needs an ending like **-ed** or **-ing**, the final consonant is usually doubled.

stop changes to **stopped**	**swim** changes to **swimming**
quit changes to **quitter**	**star** changes to **starry**

I Before E ● Rule: Use **i** before **e** except right after **c** or when rhyming with "say" as in *neighbor* or *weigh*.

* *i* before *e* words: **friend, piece, relief, believe, audience, chief, fierce**
* exceptions to *i* before *e* words: **either, neither, their, height, weird**

Silent E ● If a word ends with a silent **e**, drop the **e** before adding an ending that begins with a vowel, like **-ed** or **-ing**.

share changes to **shared**	**care** changes to **caring**

A History of the English Language

English is related to other languages, just like we are related to other people. In some ways, we look or sound like our parents and grandparents. English looks and sounds like its relatives, too. The closest language relatives—especially German and French—have helped make English what it is today. But there's more to learn about the history of English.

The Roots of Our Language

The story about English really began more than 2,000 years ago with a tribe of people in Britain called the Celts. The Celtic language, if we heard it today, would not sound like English. The Celts' language changed as it mixed with other languages to form the English of today.

From Romans to Normans

The Romans invaded Britain in A.D. 43. They stayed for a while and left behind roads, buildings, and, most importantly, the Roman alphabet. The same one we use today!

About 500 years later, three German tribes—the Angles, Saxons, and Jutes—crossed over the North Sea to Britain. Of course, they brought a lot of German words. They pushed the Celts out of the way, but mixed the languages together. Since the Angle tribe was the biggest, the country became known as Angleland, or England.

In A.D. 1066, the Normans invaded England from France. The Normans spoke French. As they lived in England, they began to use English. They added some French words like *hotel* and *nation* to feel more at home.

English in the Middle Ages

Some of the first readers and writers in England were priests and scholars. They liked to use Greek and Latin. As English became more popular, they added Greek and Latin words to the language.

At this time, people in different places spoke English differently. The invention of printed books in the 1400's changed that. Most books were printed in London. As people read more, they learned London English. Before long, many people were using the same kind of English.

English in America

When English people came to North America, they brought their language. The Native Americans, who were already here, added more words to English. They added words like *moccasin, raccoon*, and *skunk*. Native people from Central America added words like *tomato, chocolate,* and *hurricane*. Later, the Spanish-speaking people who came to America added words like *ranch* and *alligator*.

New Words

New inventions and new ways of thinking have also added words to our language. Over time, *stagecoach*, *telephone*, and *software* have become part of the language.

Today, English is a language of 500,000 words. And of course, our language will continue to grow as the world changes.

English from Around the World

Words from many languages have been added to English. This chart shows you some of these words.

Old English
man, woman
morning, night
day, month, year
cat, dog, house
red, yellow
at, in, by, from
cow, calf, pig

Scandinavian
they, them, their
knife, sky, ski
happy, scare, egg

French
constitution, city
state, nation
congress, mayor
poetry, art
court, medicine
dance, fashion
tailor, physician
beef, veal, pork

Greek
paragraph, school
alphabet
stomach

Latin
camp, wine
paper, perfume
umbrella, mile
senator, legislator

Native American
canoe
toboggan
opossum, moose
chipmunk
pecan, hickory
igloo, kayak

Spanish
cigar, mosquito
tornado
rodeo, canyon

Italian
spaghetti, pizza
macaroni
balcony, bank
piano, balloon
tarantula
volcano

Dutch
cookie, coleslaw
deck, dock
boss, pump

German
hamburger
kindergarten
pretzel, book

Asian
pepper, panther
shampoo, silk
tea, jungle
ketchup

Australian
kangaroo

African
chimpanzee
banana
banjo, okra

Middle Eastern
candy, cotton
coffee, sugar
spinach, tiger

Improving Speaking and Listening

Learning to View

Some people feel that instead of watching TV you should read a good book or play with your little sister. So what do they know? There are a lot of good things on TV, especially programs that help you understand the world around you.

Seeing the World

Just think of all the things you can see on TV:

* important events
* interesting people
* new places
* strange animals
* surprising discoveries
* natural disasters

This chapter will help you watch programs that report on important people, places, and events. You will also learn the real story behind commercials.

Watching News Programs

Some **news programs** cover news in your community and state. Other programs cover national and world news. Here are three things to remember about the news.

1. News programs can't show you everything that happens each day. That would take up too much time. Instead, the program directors must select a few events (maybe three or four) to show you.

2. News programs can't always tell the whole story for each event. If the reporters tell you too much about one story, they may not have time to tell you about other stories.

3. News reporters don't always know all of the facts. Keep watching. The facts usually become clearer over time.

Covering the Basic Facts

A good news story should tell you all the basic facts:

Who?	Third-grader Leslie Smythe
What?	rode her bike around the world
When?	last week.
Where?	She started out in Philadelphia.
Why?	She wanted to see if she could do it.
How?	Leslie's dad is an airline pilot. Leslie and her bike were on an airplane!

Watching TV Specials

TV specials give information about one subject. TV specials can be about people, places, animals, or events. You've probably watched many nature specials. You may also have seen special programs about famous events and strange creatures like Big Foot and the Loch Ness Monster. Here are some tips that will help you with your viewing.

Before Viewing

Before watching a special program, decide what you would like to know about this subject.

If your teacher gives you questions to answer, make sure you understand all of them.

During Viewing

As you watch the program, write down a few key words to help you remember important ideas.

After Viewing

Talk about the program with someone else who has watched it. Or answer your teacher's questions. (You could also write about the program in your journal.)

Watching Commercials

If you are a regular TV watcher, you see about 400 commercials every week! A surprising number, isn't it?

Commercials pay for most of the programs you watch on TV. Let's say a candy company runs commercials during a cartoon program. The company has to pay the network (ABC, CBS, Fox, etc.) to show these commercials. The network then uses this money to make or pay for the cartoon.

Selling Methods

In most cases, the people who put commercials together have one goal in mind—to get you to buy things. They use many different methods to make you believe that their products are great. Here are some of those methods:

BANDWAGON: Some commercials show a whole group of people enjoying a certain product. After watching this type of commercial, you may feel like buying the product, too. In other words, you may be ready to hop on the bandwagon.

NAME-CALLING: Instead of just saying that a product is good, some commercials say that other brands are not as good. This is a form of name-calling: Our stuff is better than all of the other stuff.

More Methods

SHOW-AND-TELL: Some commercials show how a product works. A commercial may show how easy it is to perform tricks with a new Frisbee. It's so easy even you can do it!

FAMOUS FACES: Putting famous people in commercials helps sell products. *Troy Aikmann wears _____ shoes so you should, too.* This is the famous-face method.

FACTS PLUS: A commercial may use facts to sell a product. *Nine out of 10 kids say _____ is their favorite bubble gum.* So you better try some yourself!

BEFORE AND AFTER: Let's say a commercial shows a student having a bad day at school. Then we see the same student all smiles after someone hands him a _____ candy bar. This is the old before-and-after idea: Our product will make you happy.

Learning to Listen

You spend a lot of your time listening. You listen to your teacher, your friends, your parents—even your TV! But listening is not the same as hearing. You may hear your brother talking on the phone, but you're not listening unless you pay attention and think about what he's saying.

Hearing	**vs.**	**Listening**
A dog barking		A friend telling you a story
An airplane flying		Your teacher helping you
The TV in the next room		The TV you're watching

Are You Listening?

Listening is a great way to learn things. The better you listen, the more you'll learn. At the same time, being a good listener is not easy to do. You cannot daydream or listen just when you want to. You must follow all of a speaker's words. For more listening tips, read the next page.

How to Be a Good Listener

Here are some tips that will help you become a good listener. You can use these tips whether you're listening to a friend, a parent, or your teacher.

- **Look at the person who is speaking.**
  Don't stare out the window.
  Your mind goes where your eyes go!

- **Give the speaker your full attention.**
  Listen carefully to every word.

- **Listen for key words and phrases.**
  * The **biggest** planet is Jupiter.
  * The planet **farthest** from the sun is Pluto.

- **Listen to more than just the speaker's words.**
  Decide how the person feels about his or her ideas.

- **Think about what is being said.**
  What do the speaker's ideas mean to you?

- **Ask questions when you don't understand something.**
  In class, make sure to raise your hand before you ask a question.

- **Take notes.**
  But don't try to write down too much. List only important ideas.

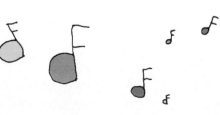

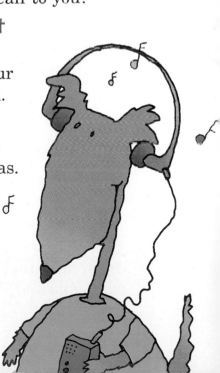

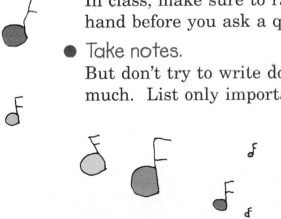

Performing
Poems

At Lola's school, a group of actors performed poems. The actors moved around and made the poems come alive. All of the students wanted the show to go on and on. They had no idea that poetry could be so much fun.

Students Onstage

Lola and some of her classmates wondered about performing poems themselves. They knew many poems and had written some of their own. (And if truth be told, they felt like hamming it up in front of their classmates!) In this chapter, we'll show you and Lola how to perform your own poems.

Moving Poetry from Page to Stage

If you follow the steps on the next four pages, your poetry performance will be a smash hit!

Forming a Team

Get together with a few classmates. A good team size is two, three, or four performers.

Finding Poems to Perform

Have you or your partners written any poems? Look them over. Look through books of poems, too—from your classroom, the library, or home.

Collect different types of poems. Take turns reading poems out loud. Collect funny ones, clever ones, and serious ones.

Choose the right poem. Poems that have a lot of action are easiest to perform, so consider those first. Poems that tell about feelings are harder, but try performing one for a challenge.

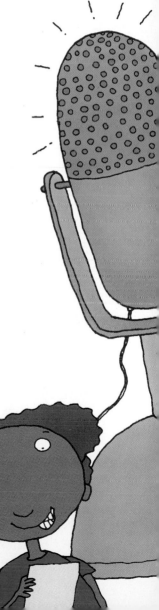

Scripting the Poem

After you have chosen a poem, divide it into speaking parts. This is called **scripting**. Let's use David L. Harrison's short poem "Show and Tell" to show you how to script. First read the poem and then see how we scripted it.

Show and Tell

Billy brought his snake to school
For show and tell today.
"This snake belongs to me," he said.
"It's gentle as can be," he said.
"It wouldn't hurt a flea," he said.
But it swallowed him anyway.

Scripted Poem ● In the scripted poem, there are two narrators (people who tell the story), Billy, and his snake.

Narrator 1:	Billy brought his snake to school
	For show and tell today.
Billy:	"This snake belongs to me,"
Narrator 2:	he said.
Billy:	"It's gentle as can be,"
Narrator 2:	he said.
Billy:	"It wouldn't hurt a flea,"
Narrator 2:	he said.
Snake:	But it swallowed him anyway.

To script your poem, you must decide how many speaking parts to include. People, animals, or things can speak. After you are finished scripting the poem, be sure all the people in your group get a copy.

Scoring the Poem

Next you must **score** the poem. That means naming feelings and movements for different lines of your script. You don't need feelings and movements for every line. Sometimes you can simply say parts of the poem.

		Feeling	**Movement**
Narrator 1:	Billy brought his snake to school For show and tell today.	*(scared)*	**biting fingernails**
Billy:	"This snake belongs to me,"	*(proud)*	**puff chest out**
Narrator 2:	he said.	*(proud)*	
Billy:	"It's gentle as can be,"	*(gentle)*	**hold out hands with pretend snake**
Narrator 2:	he said.	*(gentle)*	
Billy:	"It wouldn't hurt a flea,"	*(angry)*	**stamping feet as snake is trying to eat him**
Narrator 2:	he said.	*(angry)*	
Snake:	But it swallowed him anyway.	*(sneaky)*	**stands in front of Billy, rubbing stomach**

Performing Your Poem

After you have scripted and scored your poem, start reading it out loud. Keep practicing until everyone knows his or her lines. Then get ready to perform for real!

Five Performance Tips

- **Act confident.** Stand straight or sit tall. Don't fidget.
- **Face your audience.** As a rule, never turn your back to the audience, not even a little.
- **Introduce the poem and the poet.** Before your performance, stand shoulder to shoulder. Together, announce the title of the poem and the poet's name. Then move to your starting positions.
- **Use your "outside" voices.** This is the voice you'll need so everyone can hear you! Also remember to add the right feelings and movements when you speak.
- **Exit quietly.** When your performance is over, pause for a moment, take a bow, and return to your seats.

 Use the poem on this page for practice before you choose one of your own to perform. You will need to form a team and add your own feelings and movements to the poem. (See pages 243 and 244 for help.) Then have fun performing it!

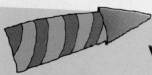

What Is a Poem
by Allan Wolf

Rocket: A Poem can be a rocket—
                     ZOOM!—that I can ride up to
                     the sky.

Bird-watcher: A Poem can be a secret room
                     where I can watch the birds
                     fly by.

Firecracker: A Poem can be loud fire-
                     works— BOOM—all whoosh
                     and bang and sparks and fun.

Flower: A Poem can be a flower bloom
                     that holds itself up to the sun.

Bird-watcher: A Poem can whisper,

Firecracker: shout,

Rocket: and play,

Flower: A Poem can dance and sing.

All: I never realized a Poem could
                     be so many things!

Giving Short Talks

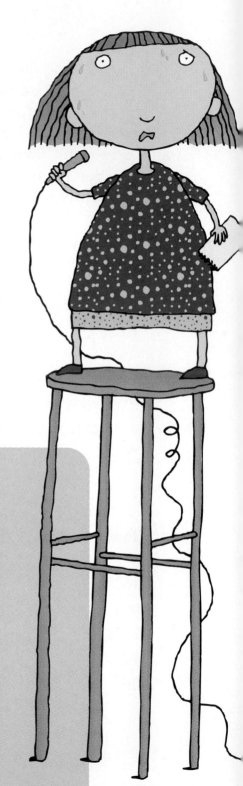

Talking is easy, isn't it? You just open your mouth and say what's on your mind . . . except when you have to talk in front of the whole class! That can be scary. You're all alone, and everybody is looking at you. What happens if your mouth won't open or your tongue falls asleep? GULP!!

Learning by Doing

Everybody feels scared at first, but giving talks becomes easier with practice. Who knows? You may even start to like it and someday become a famous talker. (Know any famous talkers?) In this part you can learn all about giving short talks—from picking a topic to practicing what you will say.

1. PICK a topic.

Pick a topic that really interests you. Here are some examples:

* Something that happened to you:
  I broke my arm.

* Something you like to do:
  I love skateboarding!

* Something you read about:
  I just read a book on whales.

Write about your topic in one sentence. Everything in your talk should be about that sentence.

2. LEARN about your topic.

You can learn about your topic by remembering, reading, and asking questions.

Remembering ● List everything that you remember and know about it. I'll bet you can fill a whole page with ideas!

Reading ● Learn more by reading about your topic. Ask your librarian about books and magazines that discuss your topic. Take notes as you read.

Asking Questions ● Talk to people who know a lot about it. If your topic is skateboarding, you could talk to someone who sells skateboards. Don't be afraid to try this. People like to share their knowledge.

3. KNOW your purpose.

Decide how or why you want to talk about your topic. This will be your purpose. Do you want to . . .

* share the important details about an event,
* help your listeners learn something new,
* make them laugh or feel sad,
* or get them to agree with you about something?

4. PLAN your talk.

Now plan what ideas you will include in your talk. The tips listed below will help you plan the beginning, the middle, and the end of your talk.

To begin your talk . . .

* say something interesting or surprising to get your listeners' attention, and
* tell what your topic is.

In the middle of your talk . . .

* give interesting facts about the topic, and
* tell how you feel about it.

To end your talk . . .

* remind listeners what your topic is, and
* repeat an important idea about it.

5. WRITE your talk.

To help you prepare for your talk, write it down on paper. There are two ways to do it. You can write the main idea on note cards. (See the sample note cards below.) Or you can write it out word for word on a full sheet of paper.

Sample Note Cards

First lines   #1

Write out the first and last lines.

Have you ever smelled a skunk? If you have, you'll never forget it! My talk is about skunks.

                                                              #2

For other cards, list important ideas.

Skunks smell bad when scared.
  – Spray a liquid.
  – It travels about
     12 feet.
  – Helps skunk say,
     "Keep away!"

6. PRACTICE giving your talk.

If you're using note cards, practice saying the ideas listed on each card. Do this over and over until all of the ideas become easy to repeat. If you have written your talk out word for word, practice reading it or try to memorize it.

Here are more practicing tips:

* As you practice, follow the tips listed in step 7.
* Start practicing early, at least two days before your talk.
* Practice in front of a few friends or family members. Ask them what they think.

7. GIVE your talk.

When you finally give your talk, follow these tips:

* Speak loudly, clearly, and slowly.
* Look at your audience. If you're reading your talk, look up often.
* Try to stand still. (We have outlawed all foot tapping and finger drumming during short talks!)

Student MODEL

Here's a short talk written by Jana Taylor.

Name the topic in an interesting way.

Give interesting facts.

Repeat the most important idea.

Skunks

Have you ever smelled a skunk? If you have, you'll never forget it! My talk is about skunks.

Skunks only smell bad when they're scared. They spray a liquid that smells awful and that can travel about 12 feet. It's the skunk's way of saying, "Keep away!" It works, too!

When you get sprayed by a skunk, you smell really bad. And it's hard to get the smell off. Our dog scared a skunk in our yard. My mom poured tomato juice all over the dog. For some reason, tomato juice helps get rid of the skunk smell.

If you've seen a skunk, it was probably a striped one. They have white stripes on their backs, and they're about the same size as a cat. But there are also spotted skunks. Spotted skunks are very small. They only weigh about one pound. When they spray they stand up on their front paws—like doing a handstand!

If you see a skunk, remember: Keep away, or you'll be smelly!

Learning to Interview

Third-grader Gabi Ruiz had an assignment. Everyone in her class had to write a report about what they wanted to be when they grew up. Gabi's uncle is a sportswriter, and she thought it sounded exciting. But she wasn't sure she really knew enough about her uncle's job. She needed more information. So Gabi called Uncle Joe to ask for an interview.

What Is an Interview?

In an **interview**, one person asks questions, and the other person answers them. It is a way to collect information. The answers can be used in reports or short talks. This chapter will help you get ready for your first interview.

Before the Interview

1

Decide what you want to learn from the interview.

- Think about what your classmates might want to know.
- List questions that will help you get all of this information.
- Begin your questions with words like *how, what,* and *why.* You can learn a lot by asking questions that begin with these words.

2

Find out who knows a lot about your topic.

- Call this person and ask for an interview.
- Identify the project you are working on.
- Set a time and place to meet.

3

Gather your materials.

- Your list of questions
- Two or three pencils
- A notebook
- A tape recorder (if you want to use one)

If you can't meet with the person you want to interview, you may be able to ask your questions over the phone.

During the Interview

 **1** **Introduce yourself and get ready for the interview.** (If you have a tape recorder, ask if it is okay to use it.)

2 **Ask your questions.**

3

Listen carefully and take notes.
* Ask the person to spell names you're not sure of.
* Ask any new questions that come to mind.

4 **After your last question is answered, say thank you.**

After the Interview

 **1** **Read your notes.** Add any details that come to mind. If you used a tape recorder, listen to the tape.

Share what you learned. Write a report or give a short talk about your interview. **2**

An Interview in Action

Here are two questions Gabi asked her uncle. Her notes are included, too.

1. Why did you decide to become a sportswriter?
   loves sports and writing
2. How did you become a sportswriter?
   went to college, learned how to watch games,
   learned a lot more on the job

MODEL Interview Report

SPORTSWRITING

Someday, I want to be a sportswriter like my uncle, Joe Cotto. You have to love sports and writing to be a sportswriter.

It is not easy to become a sportswriter! First you must go to college to learn how to be a reporter. You must also learn how to watch sports events carefully.

After college, once you have a job, you learn a lot more. My uncle said, "You'll probably get your first job in the town where you live. If you're a good writer, you may be able to get a job in a bigger city. You may be able to interview famous athletes." I'd like that.

Telling Stories

Mya remembers her grandmother telling wonderful made-up stories. Sometimes the stories were funny or sad. Sometimes they were scary. But the greatest thing about the stories was how her grandmother told them. Maybe there is someone in your family who can tell great stories. Maybe that person could be you! To become a good story-teller, you will need to do four things.

Practice as much as you can. Practice makes perfect in a lot of things, including storytelling!

Read a lot of stories so you can choose the best ones to tell.

Follow the advice on the next few pages.

Enjoy yourself!

Choosing a Story

Folktales, fairy tales, legends, and tall tales are all fun to tell. Choose a story you really like and can tell in about five minutes. Stories that repeat words or lines make good choices. Listeners like to hear special words repeated. It keeps them interested in the story.

Learning the Story

 Read the story out loud three or four times in a row. Try to picture what is happening.

 Write down the first and last sentences of the story on separate note cards.

 Then write down all the main events. Use a different index card for each event. (See the next two pages for examples.)

 On some cards, add interesting things you could say or do.

* Mark words you want to say with special feeling.
* Add movements or sounds you want to make.

 Now try to memorize what's on your cards. You should be able to tell the story without looking at your notes!

Sample Note Cards

On the next two pages, you will find sample note cards for the story "Walking Catfish." (This story is on pages 260-261.) The first five cards and the very last one are included.

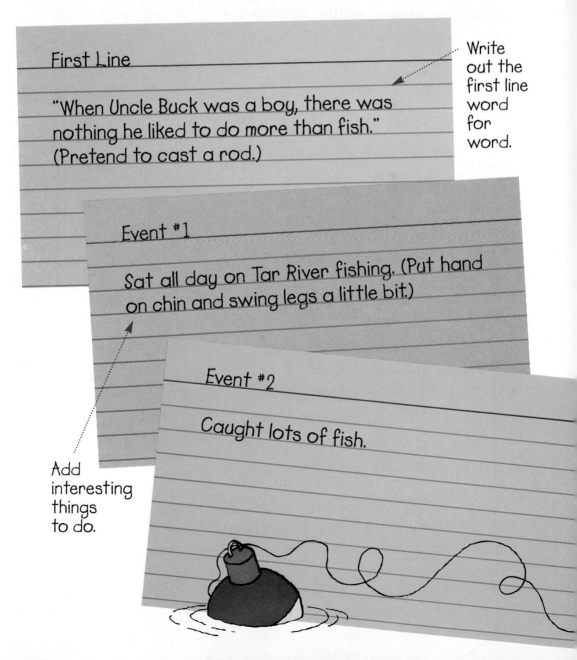

First Line

"When Uncle Buck was a boy, there was nothing he liked to do more than fish." (Pretend to cast a rod.)

Write out the first line word for word.

Event #1

Sat all day on Tar River fishing. (Put hand on chin and swing legs a little bit.)

Add interesting things to do.

Event #2

Caught lots of fish.

Event #3

Hung them all on a stringer, but one kept
breathing hard. (Say "Wooo-wheee"
three times.)

Add
interesting
things
to say.

Event #4

Buck put this fish in a water bucket and
went inside for supper. (Rub stomach.)

Last Line

"Just goes to show, ya gotta let folks be
what they're meant to be."

Write out
the last
line word
for word.

If you like "Walking Catfish," you
could write the rest of the index
cards and tell the story to someone
who has never heard it.

Professional MODEL

WALKING CATFISH
Retold by Charles Temple

When Uncle Buck was a boy, there was nothing he liked to do more than fish. Oh, he sat all day down on Tar River fishing. One July day, seemed like every time his bait hit the bottom, he felt a yank, and pulled in a big, old catfish. He'd take it off the hook, being careful not to grab the spine, and throw it up on the bank.

Buck climbed up on the bank and commenced to hang those fish on the stringer. But one hardy fellow had no intention of ending up on Buck's dinner plate. He was hangin' there breathing hard: "Wooo-wheee. Wooo-wheee. Wooo-wheee."

So Buck put him into a bucket of water and went on inside to have his supper. Next morning he come outside and took that fish out of the bucket. He was still breathing: "Wooo-wheee. Wooo-wheee. Wooo-wheee."

So Buck decided to work with him a little. He left him out of that bucket a whole hour before he put him back in. The next day, he left him out all morning. Pretty soon that fish never went back in the water at all.

Buck didn't have a puppy, so he named that fish Jake, and taught him to follow along behind him. You should have seen Jake flopping along through the dust and gravel, still breathing: "Wooo-wheee. Wooo-wheee. Wooo-wheee."

Wasn't anywhere Buck went that Jake didn't follow. Well, it turned September and the school opened up. Buck trudged off down the road to third grade. But here come Jake flopping along behind: "Wooo-wheee. Wooo-wheee. Wooo-wheee."

"Go on home, Jake," shouted Buck. "Fish can't go to school."

But Jake came on. Buck crossed that old plank bridge and walked on up to the schoolhouse. When he looked back, Buck saw a plank busted out.

He looked down in the river, and there was Jake, thrashing about like to drown.

"Swim, Jake, swim!" Buck shouted.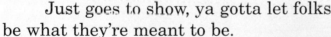
"You can do it, boy." Well, Jake took him a deep breath and dove down under the water. And you know what? Buck never saw that fish again.

Just goes to show, ya gotta let folks be what they're meant to be.

Improving Your Thinking

Getting Organized

Not much would happen without getting organized. Coaches couldn't get their teams ready. Scientists couldn't make discoveries. Cooks couldn't plan meals. Students like you couldn't do their best work. And geese would never make it south. (Well, it's important!) Getting organized is the key to success.

Gathering and Grouping Ideas

Do you have to gather your thoughts about a past event? No problem. Make a cluster. Do you have to compare two things? Try a Venn diagram. Do you have to organize a lot of facts? Write an outline.

Clusters, Venn diagrams, and outlines are called **graphic organizers**. They help you gather and group ideas. In this chapter, you will learn about these and other graphic organizers.

1. Clustering

How can you gather details about a past event? You can list ideas in any old order. Or, if you want to be more organized, you can **cluster** your ideas.

Begin clustering by writing the subject in the middle of the page. Then list related words around it. Circle and connect your words.

TIP: Clustering can help you organize facts for a report, a speech, and other projects, too.

2. Describing a Subject

How can you collect details to describe someone or something? Use a **describing wheel**. Write your subject in the middle of your wheel. List describing words on the spokes.

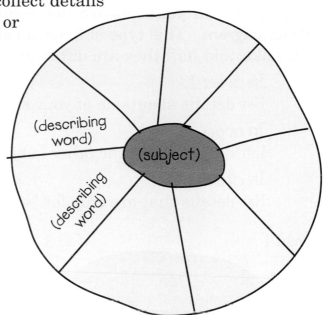

3. Answering the 5 W's

How can you tell if you know the important details about an event? Try answering the 5 W's.

TIP: You may also want to answer *How?* when you use this graphic organizer.

4. Comparing Two Subjects

How can you compare two related subjects? Use a **Venn diagram**. This type of diagram shows how two things are alike, and how they are different.

In area 1,
list details about one of your subjects.

In area 2,
list details about the other subject.

In area 3,
list details that are true for both subjects.

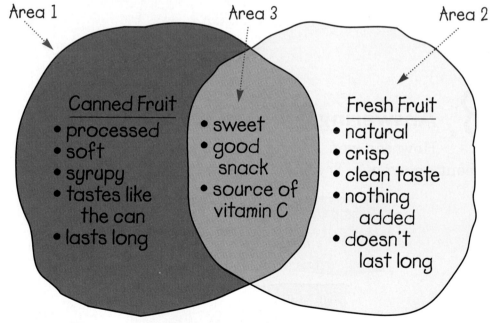

Area 1   Area 3   Area 2

Canned Fruit
- processed
- soft
- syrupy
- tastes like the can
- lasts long

- sweet
- good snack
- source of vitamin C

Fresh Fruit
- natural
- crisp
- clean taste
- nothing added
- doesn't last long

To show how two subjects are alike, use the details in area 3. To show how two subjects are different, use the details in areas 1 and 2.

5. Outlining Your Ideas

How can you organize all of the information you have collected for a speech or report? Make an **outline**.

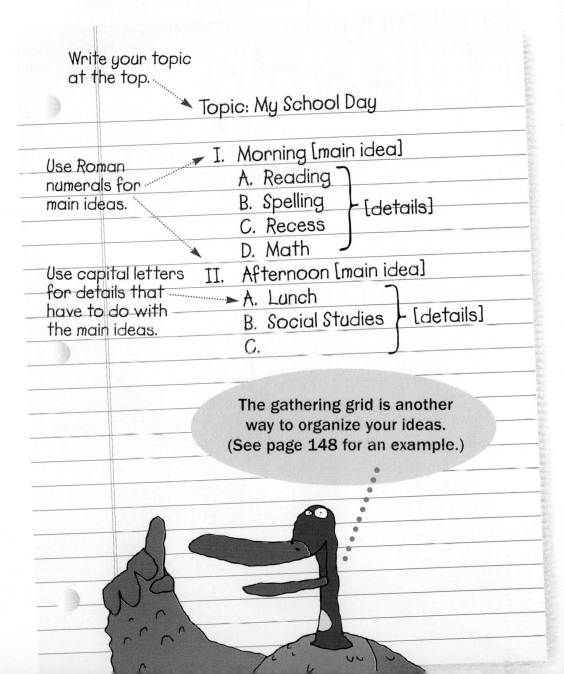

Write your topic at the top.

Topic: My School Day

I. Morning [main idea]
   A. Reading
   B. Spelling   [details]
   C. Recess
   D. Math

Use Roman numerals for main ideas.

II. Afternoon [main idea]
   A. Lunch
   B. Social Studies   [details]
   C.

Use capital letters for details that have to do with the main ideas.

The gathering grid is another way to organize your ideas. (See page 148 for an example.)

Thinking
Clearly

Let's say that you're at the mall. You and your mom get on the escalator together. But some people squeeze in between the two of you. When you get off the escalator, you can't find your mom.

Using Your Brain

The first thing you need to do is to think clearly. This chapter will tell you how to **think clearly** to solve problems, like being lost in the mall. You will also learn about thinking clearly to make decisions and to use facts and opinions correctly.

Solving Problems

Imagine you're back at the mall. You've lost your mother. What do you do?

1 **Name the problem.**

I've lost my mother in a huge mall!

2 **Think of everything you know about the problem.**

I'll never find Mom by walking around.

I can see the store where we buy cookies sometimes.

Mom said, "If you get lost, don't talk to strangers."

3 **Think of ways to solve the problem.**

I could just stay here and hope Mom finds me.

I could yell for help. But then I would have to talk to a stranger.

I could ask the man at the cookie store for help.

4 **Choose the best plan and try it out.**

I'll go to the cookie store.

5 **How did things work out?**

The man at the cookie store called security.

They said my name on the loudspeaker, and Mom came!

Making Decisions

Sometimes you have a decision to make, and you're not sure what to do. Here's how to think clearly.

 Write down what you have to decide. *Should I sign up for soccer or for swimming lessons?*

 List the facts. Also list your feelings and any questions you have.

SOCCER

Practices are on
   Thursday evenings.

Games are on Saturday
   afternoons.

I won't know anybody!

What will they teach us?

SWIMMING

Lessons are early Saturday.

I hate getting up early.

My best friend is taking
   lessons.

It could be fun with her.

What will I learn?

 Find the answers to your questions. Ask a parent or someone who has already played soccer or taken swimming lessons. Add the answers to your list.

 Make your decision. Put a ★ next to each "good" thing on your list. You might decide to do the activity with the most ★'s. Or one "good" thing—like being with your best friend—might be more important to you than anything else. It's up to you!

Using Facts and Opinions Correctly

Do you know the difference between facts and opinions? **Facts** tell something that is known to be true, or something that really happened. They tell you about the way things really are. **Opinions** are statements that someone believes. They tell you how a person thinks or feels.

FACTS

Both dogs and cats
    can be pets.

Chocolate is made
    from cacao beans.

OPINIONS

I'd rather have a
    dog than a cat.

Chocolate tastes
    great.

Know the Whole Story!

Let's say your friend calls. She says, "It snowed last night. We shouldn't have to go to school today!"

The first part of your friend's call is a fact: "It snowed last night." You can prove that statement by looking out the window. The second part is only her opinion or feeling: "We shouldn't have to go to school today." The fact is, school is open. Your mom said there were no school closings.

Opinions are fine. (A snow day would have been great!) But it's always important to know the facts before you act or react.

Sticking to the Facts

It's important to stick to the facts when you're trying to get someone to agree with you. It's also important to listen for facts when someone else wants you to agree with them! Here are four points to remember about stating facts.

A statement is not a fact just because most people agree with it.

A kangaroo would be a good classroom pet because almost everybody in the class thinks so.

No matter how many people share an opinion, it's still an opinion. It's not a fact. A kangaroo would be "hopping mad" in a classroom!

A statement is not a fact if it is based only on feelings.

A rattlesnake would be a good classroom pet because I think rattlesnakes are neat.

This statement is based on a feeling. It's not based on any facts about rattlesnakes. Here's a statement based on facts: *A rattlesnake would not be a good classroom pet because a rattlesnake bite can be deadly.*

A statement is not a fact if it is a half-truth.

If a cat scratches you, you'll get sick.

This is only half true. Most of the time, if a cat scratches you, you won't get sick. But if the cat is sick, you might get sick, too. Here's how to turn this statement into a fact: *If a cat that is sick scratches you, you might get sick, too.*

A statement is not a fact if it makes things seem worse (or better) than they really are.

When a bee stings you, it hurts so much you go crazy.

This statement makes too much out of a bee sting. (Unless, of course, you are allergic to them.) Bee stings may hurt a little. But when you put medicine on, they don't hurt for too long.

It can be hard to stick to the facts when you really want someone to agree with you. But don't get your feelings mixed up with the facts.

Writing to Learn Math

This handbook talks tons about reading and writing. But math is important, too! It is important enough to tell you how to use writing to understand math better.

Log It

Keep a learning log of thoughts and questions about math. Write notes about (1) something you just learned or (2) something you just don't get!

Here are two examples from Jacki's learning log:

April 12   Today I learned something new about multiplication. There are lots of ways to write problems that have the same answer, like 12:   12 x 1   1 x 12   2 x 6   6 x 2   3 x 4   4 x 3

April 13   I just can't remember my 9's. I always get 9 x 6 wrong. But today I taught my math partner something he didn't know! I used math cubes to show him that 6 x 7 is the same as 7 x 6. He gave me some flash cards to help me practice my 9's!

More Tips and Strategies

First Thoughts ● When you learn something new, write down what you think about it. This helps you figure out what you still need to learn about a topic.

Questions ● Write down questions you have about a topic. Don't worry about being able to answer them. Then ask your teacher or math partner to help you find answers.

Key Words ● Make a list of the important words like "subtraction" and "sum," along with their definitions.

Explanations ● Write a sentence or two that explains something you've just learned. This will help you understand it even better.

Examples ● When you're learning something new in math, write down some sample problems.

Pictures or Diagrams ● Draw pictures to make ideas clearer. For example, if you want to show how 3 x 6 is the same as 6 x 3, a picture will do it!

$12 \times 1 = 12$

$3 \times 4 = 12$

Improving Your Learning Skills

Completing Assignments

Completing assignments is a good way to learn. This chapter talks about planning ahead to get your assignments done. It also gives you tips for doing the work.

Think Ahead

Whether you have one big assignment to do, or many little assignments, planning will help. You'll have time to complete your assignments *and* do the other things you want to do.

How to Plan Ahead

▽ Each day, make a list of the assignments your teacher gives you. (See the next page.)

▷ Know exactly what you are to do for each assignment.

▽ Make sure you have everything you need: paper, pens, pencils, your books, your handbook, and so on.

▷ Plan to work on your assignments at the same time every day.

▽ Plan to work on a big assignment a little each day. (See the next page.)

△ Never rush your assignments. Try to learn as much as you can!

Tips for Doing the Work

Select a Spot ● Study in the same place each day. Pick a quiet place.

Follow Directions ● If you have a reading assignment, make sure to read the right pages!

Do the Hardest Work First ● Do the most difficult work right away, when you have the most energy.

Have a Reading Plan ● When your assignment includes reading, use a reading strategy. (See pages 200-205.)

Take Breaks ● Take breaks when you really need them. (Not every five minutes, though!)

Daily Assignment Chart

List the important information for each assignment.

Homework for Jan. 15

List pages and numbers.

Math   Do problems 5-30, page 71
            Show work ◄············· List special notes.

Social Studies Finish treasure map
                Bring home colored pencils
                                    ◄············· List supplies.

Reading   Pack mystery book ◄·············
                Start reading

Planning for Big Assignments

A chart can help you turn a big assignment into little ones. Here's one plan for writing an ABC book. (This plan only covers the first week.)

Monday   Pick a subject. List ideas for first 10 letters.
Tuesday   List ideas for other letters.
Wednesday   Learn about the letter ideas.
Thursday   Begin first draft.
Friday   Work on first draft.

Working in Groups

There are lots of things you must do in a group. (Your homework isn't one, though!) We're talking about playing soccer, putting on a play, or doing certain kinds of projects. These are activities that bring people together to work or to play.

Working Together

Sometimes you'll work with one other person. Other times, small groups of three to six people will be needed. And sometimes you'll work in large groups . . . maybe your whole class, or even your whole school. No matter how large or small your group is, it's important to get along and get the job done!

Working in Pairs

When two people work together, it's called working in pairs. You're partners!

Tips for Partners

Share Your Ideas ● Talk with each other about what you're going to do. What is your assignment? Writing a poem? Acting out a play?

Share Jobs ● Decide who will do what. If you're writing a play, for example, each partner could write the lines for different characters.

Plan Your Work ● Talk with each other about how much work you will do each day. When is the assignment due?

Listen to Each Other ● The whole idea of working together is to use two brains instead of one. Offer your ideas, and then listen to your partner's ideas.

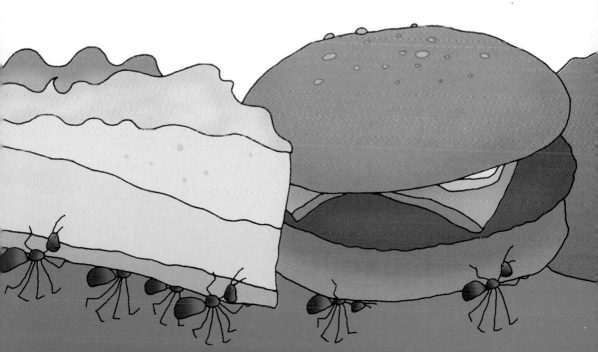

Working in Small Groups

In some ways, working in small groups is like working in pairs. You should all understand the assignment. And everybody should have a chance to talk, while the others listen carefully.

Working in small groups can be harder, though, than working in pairs. There are more people, and it can be tough to agree on things.

Tips for Group Work

Share and Write Down Ideas ● As group members share their ideas, have someone take notes. This way you'll have a list of everyone's ideas.

Take Turns ● Take turns talking about the different ideas. Say what you like about an idea, and what you don't like. It's okay to disagree in a polite way:

> This idea sounds great, but I don't think we'll have time to do it.

Plan Your Work ● Combine the best parts of different ideas into one plan that everyone agrees with. For example, if Jon wants to write a play and Sean wants to write a song, see if you can please both of them:

> Let's write a play that includes a song.

Making a Plan

Every group project should include a plan. Group members should ask themselves these questions:

* What is our project?
* When is the project due?
* What do we need to do to complete the project?
* What job or jobs will each group member do?

Use an outline like the one below to help your group make its plan. Be sure everyone agrees with the plan.

Group Plan

A. Our project is
   (Write a play? Research a topic?)

B. Our due date is

C. Things we need to do:
   1.
   2.
   3.

D. Jobs for each group member:
   Name   Job
   Name   Job
   Name   Job

Taking Tests

You may not like taking tests. But you probably don't like eating spinach or going to the dentist, either. So let's forget about what you don't like. Let's be more positive! Tests are a very important part of school. They show how much you've learned about a subject and what you still need to work on.

Getting Ready

Tests are no problem if you keep up with your class work. It also helps to prepare for each test. In this chapter, you will learn how to study for tests, how to take different types of tests, and more.

Five Smart Things to Do

1   **Listen up!**

When your teacher starts talking about your next test, forget about your growling stomach. Listen to everything she has to say. She will tell you what the test will be on and when it will be given.

2   **Gather all of your materials.**

Stuff your backpack with everything you need to study, including your textbook and all handouts.

3   **Plan your study time.**

If your test is two days away, study a little each night before the test. Don't wait until the last minute!

4   **Look over everything.**

Start with your textbook. Review the chapter page by page. Study the chapter headings and words in bold print. Also look over the review questions at the end of the chapter. Then study each handout or assignment. (See page 291 for more ideas.)

5   **Find a study partner.**

Ask someone in your family first. If you ask one of your friends, make sure this person really wants to study.

Types of Tests

Tests come in many different shapes and sizes. The five most common types are listed here. (You can learn about each type of test on the next five pages.)

True/False

Matching

Multiple Choice

Fill in the Blank

Short Answer

True/False Test

On a **true/false test**, you are given a list of sentences. After reading each one, you have to decide if it is true or false.

✳ If any part of the sentence is false, the answer is false. If the whole sentence is true, the answer is true.

✳ Watch for words like *always, never, all,* or *none.* Few things are always true or never true.

Directions: Read each sentence carefully. Then put a T before each true statement and an F before each false statement.

_____ 1. New York City is the largest city in the United States.

_____ 2. All major cities are built next to a large body of water.

Answers:

1. T

2. F – "All" is the key word that makes this statement false.

Matching Test

On a **matching test**, you are given two lists of words or phrases. You have to find the ones from each list that go together, or match.

* Before making any matches, read through both lists.
* Put a mark next to each answer you use. Then it will be easier for you to see which answers you have left.

Directions: Match the topic in the first column with the correct letter in the second column.

_____	Downtown	a. settled area near a big city
_____	Industrial Region	b. main business district in a city
_____	Suburb	c. area of factories and warehouses

Answers:

Downtown (b)
Industrial Region (c)
Suburb (a)

Multiple-Choice Test

On a **multiple-choice test**, you will be given different statements or questions with four or five choices under each one. You must select the best choice to complete the statement or answer the question.

✳ Read each statement or question very carefully. Look for words like *not, never,* or *except.* They can change the meaning of the statement.

✳ Study all of the choices. Then select the best one.

Directions: Read each statement carefully. Then select the letter that best completes each one.

1. People move to cities for many reasons, but not for
   (a) jobs   (b) events & activities   (c) peace & quiet

2. City government provides all of the following, except for
   (a) police protection   (b) grocery stores
   (c) street repair   (d) city parks

Answers:

1. (c) People do not move to cities for peace and quiet.
2. (b) City governments provide all of the choices, except for grocery stores.

Fill-in-the-Blank Test

On a **fill-in-the-blank test**, you will be given a list of sentences that you must complete. There are no choices given. You must know the right words to fill in the blanks.

* Count the number of blanks to fill in. The number of blanks usually tells you how many words should be in your answer.

* Ask yourself what information fits into the blank. Does the sentence need *a who? a what? a when?* or *a where?*

Directions: Carefully read each sentence. Then fill in the blank or blanks to make each statement complete.

1. In the United States, most people live in _____ areas.

2. _____ and _____ are the two main types of mass transit in a big city.

Answers:

1. urban
2. Buses and trains

Short-Answer Test

On a **short-answer test**, you write either sentence or paragraph answers. Here are the kinds of things you might be asked to do:

Define what something means.

Describe how something looks or sounds.

Explain how something works or what it does.

List facts about something.

Example: Describe what the tundra looks like. (Or it might be stated as a question: What is the tundra?)

Writing Tips

Read the statement or question carefully. Look for a key word like *describe*. If you don't understand the question, ask for help.

Plan your answer. Make a list of ideas to include.

- flat land
- mosses and shrubs, no trees
- frozen ground
- Arctic area

Write your answer. Your first sentence should state the subject you are writing about.

A tundra is a large, flat area of land in the Arctic. It has no trees, only mosses and small shrubs. This is because the ground under the topsoil stays frozen all the time. Nothing with deep roots can grow there.

R E M E M B E R I N G for Tests

Use a Memory Trick ● Here's one trick that really works:

> Let's say you had to remember the names of the five Great Lakes. If you put these names in a certain order, the first letters spell a word.

> Huron, Ontario, Michigan, Erie, Superior
> spells HOMES.

> HOMES will help you remember the names of the Great Lakes for the test.

Make an Idea Map ● An idea map will help you organize information.

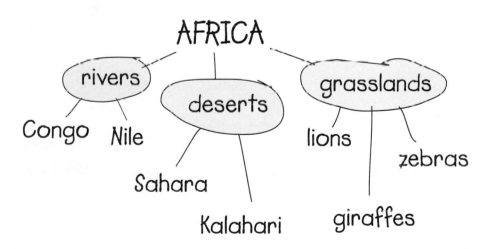

Use Flash Cards ● Write one fact on each card. Carry the cards around and read one whenever you have a chance.

4 The Proofreader's Guide

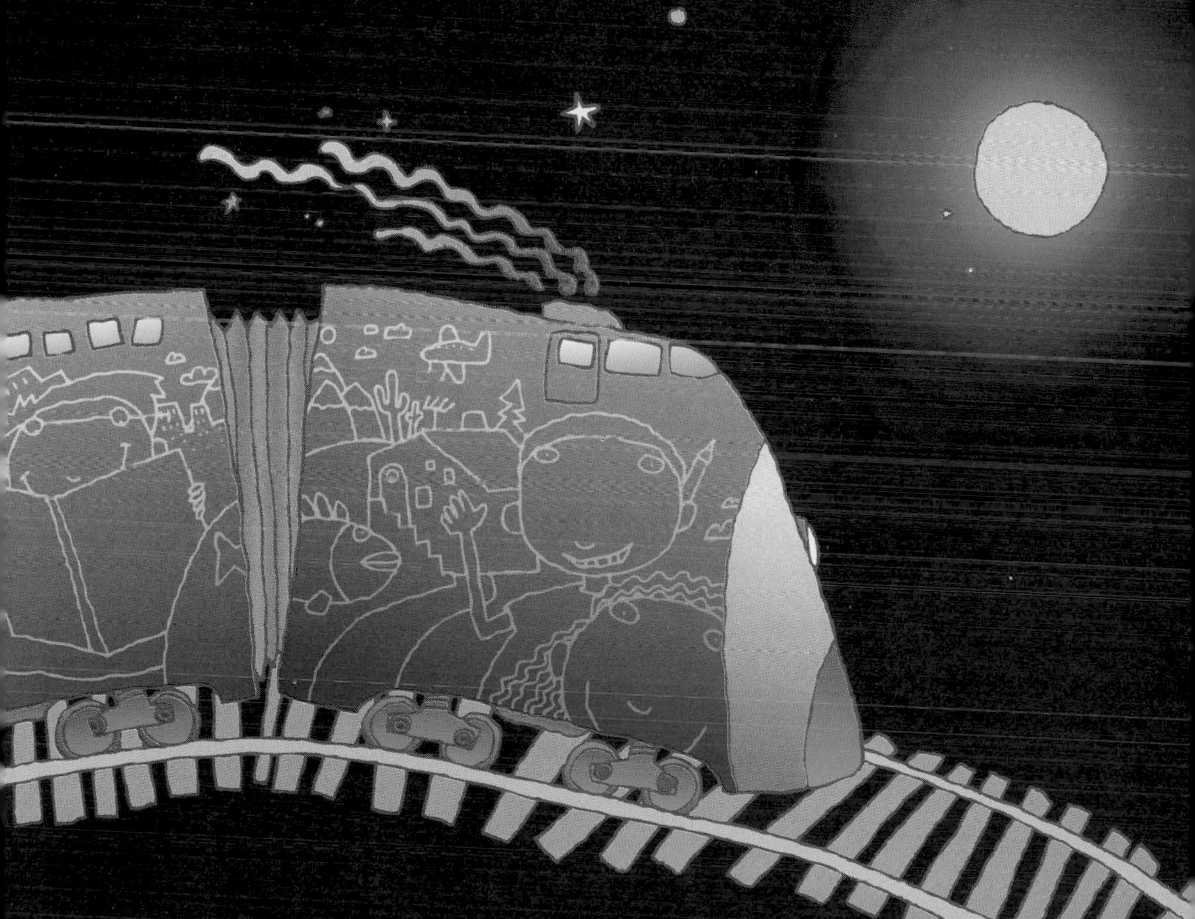

Proofreader's Guide

Using Punctuation

Punctuation marks are very important. They help make your ideas clear. Just think what your writing would be like without them. All of your words and ideas would run together like water. It would not be a pretty sight.

The first part of the "Proofreader's Guide" gives you all of the rules for punctuation marks. Turn to this chapter whenever you have a question about putting the right punctuation in
the right place.

On Your Mark

Here's what you'll find in this section:

Period

A **period** is used at the end of a sentence. It has other important uses, too.

You've been using periods ever since you started writing. ◀········

period

At the End of a Sentence

● A period is used at the end of a sentence that makes a statement.

We use the computer every day. (statement)

● A period is also used at the end of a request.

Please turn off the computer. (request)

After an Initial

● A period is used after an initial in a person's name.

L. Frank Baum   A. A. Milne   B. B. King

After an Abbreviation

● A period is used after an abbreviation that shortens a word.

Ms.   Mrs.   Mr.   Dr.   Jr.   W. First St.

As a Decimal in a Number

● Use a period as a decimal point in numbers.

My mother said my temperature is 99.6 degrees.

● Use a period to separate dollars and cents.

It costs $2.50 to see a movie.

Comma

Commas tell a reader where to rest or pause in a sentence. They are used to make your writing easier to read.

A comma looks like a period with a tail on it (,).

comma

To Separate Items in a Series

● Use a comma between words or phrases in a series. A series is a list of three or more things.

I like pizza, pickles, and pretzels. **(words)**

Garfield eats tons of food, talks smart to Jon, and plays tricks on Odie. **(phrases)**

In Letter Writing

● Use a comma after the greeting in a friendly letter.
Dear Auntie Liz,   **(greeting)**

● Use a comma after the closing in all letters.
Yours truly, **(closing)**
Sally

To Keep Numbers Clear

● Use a comma in large numbers of four or more digits.
He says his card collection is worth $1,000!
We collected 22,000 soda cans in our school.

Comma

Between a City and a State

● Use a comma between a city and a state in a sentence or in an address.

He moved to Sleepy Hollow, New York. **(sentence)**

110 Hill Street **(address)**
Hannibal, MO 53401

TIP: Do not use a comma between a state and a ZIP code.

Between the Day and the Year in a Date

● Use a comma between the day and the year in a sentence or in the heading of a letter.

I saw Uncle Sam on July 4, 1995.

701 Liberty Street
Fredonia, WI 53021
July 4, 1995

In a Compound Sentence

● Use a comma before the connecting word in a compound sentence. A compound sentence is made up of two simple sentences connected by *or, and,* or *but.*

I will feed Linus, but I won't clean his litter box!

Linus ran away once, and we looked everywhere for him.

Comma

To Set Off a Speaker's Words in a Sentence

● Use a comma to set off the exact words of a speaker from the rest of the sentence.

Maddie said, "If I have four eggs and you have six eggs, what do we get when we put them together?"

"Ten eggs," said her mother.

"No," Maddie said, "we get scrambled eggs!"

After an Introductory Word

A Word That Shows Surprise ● Use a comma to set off an interjection. An interjection is a word that shows surprise.

Wow, you hit that ball a mile!

Hey, will you show me how to do that?

The Name of a Person Spoken To ● Use a comma to set off the name of someone you are speaking to.

Mom, what's in this casserole?

Todd, may I have your Jell-O?

Between Describing Words

● Use a comma between two words that describe the same noun.

His pet is a hairy, black spider!

I like wearing big, floppy hats.

Colon

A **colon** is used in three special cases, including how to show time. (You won't use this punctuation mark very often.)

To make a colon, put one dot on top of another one (:).

colon

Between Numbers in Time

● A colon is used between the parts of a number that show time.

My school starts at 7:45 a.m.

I'll meet you on the playground at 3:30.

In a Business Letter

● A colon is used after the salutation in a business letter.

Dear Ms. Yolen: Dear Editor:

Dear Mr. Wilson: Dear Office Manager:

To Introduce a List

● A colon may be used to introduce a list.

I don't like to do these things: take showers, do homework, and go to bed early.

Here are my favorite foods: pizza, spaghetti, and pancakes.

Apostrophe

An **apostrophe** is used to make contractions or to show ownership.

An apostrophe looks like a comma,
but it is placed between letters like this: It's lunchtime!

apostrophe

In Contractions

● An apostrophe is used to form a contraction. The apostrophe takes the place of one or more letters.

Contraction	Short For	Contraction	Short For
don't	do not	they're	they are
isn't	is not	you're	you are
it's	it is; it has	wasn't	was not

To Show Ownership (Possessives)

Singular Possessive ● An apostrophe plus an *s* is added to a singular noun to show ownership. (Singular means "one.")

My friend's dog ate the dish of food. Then it ate the dish!

Plural Possessive ● An apostrophe is usually added after the *s* in a plural noun to show ownership. (Plural means "more than one.")

The girls' team beat the boys' team in the race.

For plural nouns not ending in *s*, an apostrophe plus an *s* must be added.

My mice's cage is a mess!

Quotation Marks

Quotation marks are used to punctuate titles and to set off a speaker's exact words. Remember that quotation marks always come in pairs. One set comes before the quoted words, and one set comes after them like this:

Porky Pig says, "That's all, folks!"

quotation marks

To Punctuate Titles

● Quotation marks are used to punctuate titles of songs, poems, and short stories.

> We sang "The Lion Sleeps Tonight" in music class.
>
> Ms. Barr read a poem called "Whispers."
>
> Tommie read a story called "Swamp Monster."

Before and After Spoken Words

● Quotation marks are used before and after the exact words of the speaker in a sentence.

> "What's that?" I asked.
>
> My dad said, "It's just a pile of old gray rags."
>
> "Dad," I asked, "can gray rags have a pink nose?"
>
> Finally, Dad looked carefully into the chicken coop. "It's a possum! We just woke up a sleeping possum."

TIP: In almost all cases, punctuation is placed inside quotation marks. (Study the model above.)

Hyphen

To Divide a Word

- A **hyphen** is used to divide words. Hyphens come in handy when you run out of room at the end of a line.

hyphen

> Hawks eat many things. They really like mice, grass-
> hoppers, and even snakes. A hawk kills a mouse by grabbing
> onto it with its claws and shaking it.

TIP: Divide words only between syllables. (The word *grass-hop-per* can be divided in two places.)

In Fractions

- A hyphen is used between the numbers in written fractions.

> I lost one-half of my allowance!

Question Mark

At the End of a Question

- A **question mark** is used at the end of a direct question.

> Who put the hot sauce on my taco?
> Will I ever be able to taste again?

question mark

Exclamation Point

To Express Strong Feeling

- An **exclamation point** is used to express strong feeling. It may be placed after a word, a phrase, or a sentence.

  Awesome! ◄·············· exclamation point

  Happy birthday! (phrase)

  There's a brontosaurus! (sentence)

  TIP: Don't use too many exclamation points in your writing. They lose their value when they are used again and again.

Parentheses

To Add Information

- **Parentheses** are used to add information. Parentheses always come in pairs.

  ·······parentheses

  The map (see figure 2) will help you understand the trail.

  When you find important information, write down only the main ideas. (This is called note taking.)

Underlining (Italics)

To Mark Titles

● **Underlining** is used to mark titles of books, plays, television programs, movies, and magazines. If you use a computer, you can put titles in *italics* instead of underlining them.

underlining   italics

The Ghostmobile or *The Ghostmobile* (a book)

The Lion King (a movie)

Nature (a television program)

A Woman Called Truth (a play)

Sports Illustrated for Kids (a magazine)

TIP: Remember that you use quotation marks (" ") for titles of short stories, poems, and songs.

For Special Words

● Underlining (or italics) is used to mark the names of aircraft and ships.

Merrimac or *Merrimac* (Civil War ship)

Discovery or *Discovery* (spacecraft)

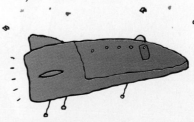

Checking Mechanics

You know all about capitalizing the first word in a sentence. And you know about capitalizing specific names (Abbie, Alabama). But what other words need capital letters? You can find out on the next few pages. Capitalizing words is easy if you know where to look for help.

This chapter will also help you write plurals of nouns and use numbers and abbreviations correctly. In other words, all of the sticky little problems of **mechanics** are covered here. Your writing will run smoothly if you follow the rules and examples on the next seven pages.

Mechanics Tools

Capitalization ▶ **307**
Plurals ▶ **310**
Numbers ▶ **311**
Abbreviations ▶ **312**

Capitalization

Proper Nouns and Proper Adjectives

● Capitalize all proper nouns and proper adjectives. A proper noun names a specific person, place, or thing. Proper adjectives are formed from proper nouns.

Jacksonville Jaguars (proper noun)

Beverly Cleary (proper noun)

California raisins (proper adjective)

the Spanish language (proper adjective)

Words Used as Names

● Capitalize words such as *mother, father, aunt,* and *uncle* when these words are used as names.

Dad asked us to go to the mall with Mom and him.

If Dad goes, Uncle Terry will go, too.

(No capital letter is needed if you say *my* mother, *your* dad, and so on.)

Titles Used with Names

● Capitalize titles used with names.

President Abraham Lincoln   Mr. Ramirez

Dr. Martin Luther King, Jr.   Mayor Barbara Long

TIP: Do not capitalize titles when they are used alone: the president, the doctor, the mayor.

Capitalization

Abbreviations

● Capitalize abbreviations of titles and organizations.

Mr. (Mister)

ABC (American Broadcasting Company)

NFL (National Football League)

Titles

● Capitalize the first word of a title, the last word, and every important word in between.

Highlights for Children (magazine)

"When You Wish upon a Star" (song)

Beauty and the Beast (movie)

When I Was Young in the Mountains (book)

First Words

● Capitalize the first word of every sentence.
The first day at a new school is not easy.

● Capitalize the first word of a direct quotation.
The teacher said, "Welcome to my class, Jamin."

Days and Months

● Capitalize the names of days of the week, months of the year, and special holidays.

Friday   April   Fourth of July   Arbor Day   Thanksgiving

(Do not capitalize the seasons: **winter, spring, summer, fall.**)

Capitalizing Geographic Names

Planets and heavenly bodies ....**Earth, Mars, Milky Way**

Continents...........................**Europe, Asia, Africa, North America**

Countries..................**Canada, Mexico, United States of America**

States............................**Utah, Ohio, Washington, Maine, Indiana**

Provinces...............**Yucatan, Chihuahua, Quebec, Newfoundland**

Cities and counties.....................................**Buffalo, New York City,
Mexico City, Los Angeles County**

Bodies of water ....**Red Sea, Lake Michigan,
Mississippi River, Atlantic Ocean,
Gulf of Mexico, St. Lawrence Seaway**

Landforms................................**Rocky Mountains, Mount Everest,
Hawaiian Islands**

Public areas...**Statue of Liberty Island,
Yellowstone National Park**

Streets, roads, and highways ....**Santa Monica Freeway,
Main Street, Rock Road, Skyline Drive,
Park Avenue, Interstate 95**

Buildings.................................**Sears Tower, World Trade Center,
Petronas Towers**

Capitalize	Do Not Capitalize
January, October...winter, fall	
Mother (as a name)...........................my mother (describing her)	
President Clinton ....Bill Clinton, our president	
Mayor Hefty..Ms. Hefty, our mayor	
Lake Erie ....the lake area	
the South (section of the country) ....south (a direction)	
planet Earth ....the earth we live on	

Plurals

- Plurals of most nouns are made by adding an *s*.

    balloon – balloons   shoe – shoes

Nouns Ending in *sh, ch, x, s,* and *z*

- The plurals of nouns ending in *sh, ch, x, s,* and *z* are made by adding *es* to the singular.

    wish – wishes   lunch – lunches   box – boxes

    dress – dresses   buzz – buzzes

Nouns Ending in *y*

- The plurals of common nouns that end in *y* (with a consonant letter just before the *y*) are formed by changing the *y* to *i* and adding *es*.

    sky – skies   story – stories   puppy – puppies

- The plurals of nouns that end in *y* (with a vowel before the *y*) are formed by adding only *s*.

    day – days   monkey – monkeys   toy – toys

Irregular Nouns

- Some nouns form a plural by taking on an irregular spelling.

    child – children
    mouse – mice
    goose – geese

Numbers

Writing Numbers

● Numbers from one to nine are usually written as words; all numbers 10 and over are usually written as numerals.

one   four   23   45   365   5,280

Except: Numbers being compared should be kept in the same style.

Students from 6 to 10 years old are invited.

Very Large Numbers

● You may use a combination of numbers and words for very large numbers.

17 million   1.5 billion

Sentence Beginnings

● Use words, not numerals, to begin a sentence.

Nineteen students in the class had brown hair.

Numerals Only

● Use numerals for any numbers in the following forms:

money .... $1.50   **decimal** 98.6

percentage .... 50 percent   **page** .... pages 12-21

chapter .... chapter 5   **address** .... 701 Hill Street

date .... June 6   **time** .... 3:30 p.m.

statistic .... a score of 5 to 2

Abbreviations

Abbreviations

● An abbreviation is the shortened form of a word or phrase. Most abbreviations begin with a capital letter and end with a period.

Mrs.   Mr.   Dr.   Ave.   a.m.   p.m.   adj. (adjective)

● Days of the week

Sun. (Sunday)   Wed. (Wednesday)   Sat. (Saturday)

Mon. (Monday)   Thurs. (Thursday)

Tues. (Tuesday)   Fri.   (Friday)

● Months of the year

Jan. (January)   May   (May)   Sept. (September)

Feb. (February)   Jun. (June)   Oct. (October)

Mar. (March)   Jul. (July)   Nov. (November)

Apr. (April)   Aug. (August)   Dec. (December)

Acronyms and Initialisms

● An acronym (*say* à-krə-nim) is a word formed from the first letter or letters of words in a phrase.

MADD (Mothers Against Drunk Driving)

● An initialism is like an acronym, but the initials (letters) are not pronounced as a word.

CD (**c**ompact **d**isc)

STATE ABBREVIATIONS

	Standard	Postal		Standard	Postal
Alabama	Ala.	AL	Missouri	Mo.	MO
Alaska	Alaska	AK	Montana	Mont.	MT
Arizona	Ariz.	AZ	Nebraska	Neb.	NE
Arkansas	Ark.	AR	Nevada	Nev.	NV
California	Calif.	CA	New Hampshire	N.H.	NH
Colorado	Colo.	CO	New Jersey	N.J.	NJ
Connecticut	Conn.	CT	New Mexico	N.M.	NM
Delaware	Del.	DE	New York	N.Y.	NY
District of			North Carolina	N.C.	NC
Columbia	D.C.	DC	North Dakota	N.D.	ND
Florida	Fla.	FL	Ohio	Ohio	OH
Georgia	Ga.	GA	Oklahoma	Okla.	OK
Hawaii	Hawaii	HI	Oregon	Ore.	OR
Idaho	Idaho	ID	Pennsylvania	Pa.	PA
Illinois	Ill.	IL	Rhode Island	R.I.	RI
Indiana	Ind.	IN	South Carolina	S.C.	SC
Iowa	Iowa	IA	South Dakota	S.D.	SD
Kansas	Kan.	KS	Tennessee	Tenn.	TN
Kentucky	Ky.	KY	Texas	Tex.	TX
Louisiana	La.	LA	Utah	Utah	UT
Maine	Maine	ME	Vermont	Vt.	VT
Maryland	Md.	MD	Virginia	Va.	VA
Massachusetts	Mass.	MA	Washington	Wash.	WA
Michigan	Mich.	MI	West Virginia	W. Va.	WV
Minnesota	Minn.	MN	Wisconsin	Wis.	WI
Mississippi	Miss.	MS	Wyoming	Wyo.	WY

ADDRESS ABBREVIATIONS

Avenue	Ave.	AVE	North	N.	N
Boulevard	Blvd.	BLVD	Road	Rd.	RD
Court	Ct.	CT	South	S.	S
Drive	Dr.	DR	Square	Sq.	SQ
East	E.	E	Street	St.	ST
Highway	Hwy.	HWY	West	W.	W

TIP: Use postal abbreviations when addressing envelopes.

Checking Your Spelling

This spelling list includes many of the important and useful words you will use in your writing. Check this list when you are unsure of the spelling of a certain word. (Also check your own spelling dictionary or a classroom dictionary.)

A

about
afraid
after
again
almost

alone
always
angry
animal
another
answer
anybody

April
aren't
asked
asleep
August
aunt
author

See pages 224-227 for tips on becoming a better speller.

Write on Track

B

bear
beautiful
because
behind
believe
better
blood
body
both
bought
break
breakfast
bright
built
bunch
bushes

C

captain
care
catch
caught
cause
change
cheese
children
climb
clothes
could
country
cousin
cover
crazy

D

dance
daughter
dead
dear
December
decided
desk
didn't
different
dirty
doesn't
dressed
drive
dropped
dumb
during

E

early
earth
either
engine
enough
everyone
everything

F

famous
favorite
February
few
field
fight

finally
finger
finished
first
flew
floor
flying
folks
follow
forest
forget
forgive
fought
Friday
front

G

ghost
giant
grade
ground
group
guess
gym

H

half
happen
happiness
heard
heart
hello
high
honey
hospital

huge
hungry
hurry
hurt

I

idea
I'll
I'm
important
inches
inside
instead
interest
island
isn't
it's

J

jail
January
join
July
June

K

kept
kitchen
knew
knife
knocked
know

L

laugh
learn
leave
library
listen
loose
loud
lunch

M

machine
mail
March
May
maybe
metal
middle
might
minute
mirror
Monday
monster
mouse
mouth
movie
music

N

near
neighbor
nobody
noise

north
nothing
November

O

ocean
o'clock
October
often
once
orange
other
outside
own

P

paint
paper
parents
past
pencil
people
person
phone
picture
piece
planet
pleased
police
poor
power
president
pretty
probably

Q

question
quick
quiet

R

reached
ready
really
reason
remember
report
rest
right
river
rocket
rough
round

S

Saturday
scared
science
scream
secret
September
sight
since
small
someone
something
special
spring
stairs

strange
strong
Sunday
sure
surprise

T

taught
their
thought
threw
through
Thursday
together
tonight
toward
trouble
truth
Tuesday

U

uncle
understand
until
upon
usual

V

visit
voice

W

wasn't
watch
wear
weather
Wednesday
which
whole
window
winter
without
woman
women
word
world
worry
would
wrong

X

X ray
xylophone

Y

young
you're

Z

zero

Using the Right Word

This chapter lists common homophones (*say* `hä-mə-fōnz`). Homophones are words that sound the same but have different spellings or meanings like *to, too,* and *two.* If you know the common homophones, you won't make a mistake like this in your writing:

I blue my nose.

Sounds like someone painted his or her nose, doesn't it? *Blew* is the right word to use.

ant, aunt	**Ants** are insects that work hard. **It's a blast when my aunt baby-sits for us.**
ate, eight	**I ate the teacher's apple.** **My friend had eight pieces of licorice.**
bare, bear	**She tested the water with her bare feet.** **Watch for bears when you pick berries.**

blew, blue	The guy next to me blew his nose. The ocean is blue because of the sky.
brake, break	His bicycle has a bad brake. It will break if he presses on it too hard.
buy, by	I need to buy a new lamp. Did that light go on all by itself?
cent, scent, sent	I bought a total of 99 balloons for 99 cents. The candle has a pine scent. He sent her a birthday card.
close, clothes	Close the door. Put the clothes in the dryer.
creak, creek	Old boats creak when they move. The water in the creek smells funny.
dear, deer	Jasmine is my dear friend. Deer come out of the woods to feed.
dew, do, due	You'll find dew on the grass in the morning. I do my homework right away. My report is due today.
eye, I	Sam wore an eye patch to look like a pirate. I played the part of the captain.
for, four	I always pick popcorn for a snack. My four brothers love chips and salsa.

hare, hair	**A hare looks like a large rabbit.** **My hair sometimes looks like a wet rabbit.**
heal, heel	**It takes about a week for a cut to heal.** **The heel of my shoe came off!**
hear, here	**I can't hear you.** **I was right here all of the time.**
heard, herd	**I heard the noise from the street.** **It sounded like a herd of buffalo!**
hole, whole	**My basketball has a hole in it.** **That ruined my whole day.**
hour, our	**The assembly lasted one hour.** **Our class sat in the front row.**
its, it's	**Our class needs its sharpener fixed.** **It's eating all our pencils.** (It's = It is)
knew, new	**I knew everyone's name on the first day.** **A new girl named Vanessa has green eyes.**
knight, night	**The knight put on his armor.** **He can't go out at night.**
know, no	**Do you know how this thing works?** **No, I'll have to ask my teacher.**

made, maid	**Who made this mess?** **Cinderella was a maid.**
main, mane	**My main skill is fly catching.** **The lion's mane needs brushing.**
meat, meet	**My older sister doesn't eat meat.** **I will meet her at the health food store.**
one, won	**The pitcher threw one ball and two strikes.** **They won the game in the last inning.**
pair, pare, pear	**The pair of shoes had orange laces.** **Machines can pare apples in 10 seconds.** **A pear is a fruit a little bit like an apple.**
peace, piece	**Who likes peace and quiet?** **Alex got the biggest piece of cake.**
plain, plane	**Grandma likes plain toast for breakfast.** **Buffalo eat the long grass on the plain.** **The stunt plane flew upside down.**
read, red	**Have you read any books by Jane Yolen?** **Why do you always eat the red M&M's?**
right, write	**He must have said turn right!** **Next time, I'll write down the directions.**
road, rode, rowed	**I saw a covered bridge on a country road.** **My sister rode my bike all day.** **We rowed the boat to the island.**

scene, seen	The movie shows great mountain scenes. Have you seen mountains before?
sea, see	A sea is like an ocean. I can't see anything in the dark.
sew, so, sow	My brother had to sew the sail. Get in so we can get going! Each spring we sow seeds in our garden.
soar, sore	Hawks soar high in the air. One hawk had a sore wing.
some, sum	I have some good news and some bad news. The sum of two numbers is the total.
son, sun	My grandpa is the son of a baker. The sun is only 93 million miles from us.
tail, tale	Did you ever step on a cat's tail? My teacher told a tall tale about Pecos Bill.
their, there, they're	The girls won their soccer game. (*Their* shows ownership.) There are 12 girls on the team. Now they're the champs. (they're = they are)
threw, through	He threw the Frisbee. It sailed right through the open window.

to, two, too	**We went to the zoo.**
	We took two buses.
	Daryl ate too much food.
	(*Too* means "more than enough" or "very.")
	I ate a lot of food, too. (*Too* means "also.")
waist, waste	**She wore a yellow belt around her waist.**
	Put the trash in the waste bin.
wait, weight	**We had to wait 20 minutes.**
	Our dog has to lose weight.
way, weigh	**Am I going the right way?**
	I want to weigh my cat.
weak, week	**My skinny arms are weak.**
	Next week I'll start exercising.
wear, where	**Which baseball cap should I wear?**
	Where are you going?
which, witch	**Which book should I read?**
	I like The Lion, the Witch, and the Wardrobe.
wood, would	**The doghouse was made of wood.**
	Would Mugsy like it?
your, you're	**Pick up your clothes before Mom gets home.**
	(*Your* shows ownership.)
	You're right about my room. (You're = You are)

Understanding Sentences

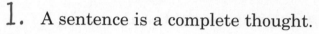

Important Things to Know About Sentences

1. A sentence is a complete thought.

2. A sentence has two basic parts—a subject and a predicate (verb).

3. A sentence makes a statement, asks a question, gives a command, or shows strong emotion.

4. A sentence begins with a capital letter and ends with a period, a question mark, or an exclamation point.

5. You can find more about sentences on the next three pages and on pages 69-73.

Sentence Guide
Parts of a
Sentence ▶ **325**

Types of
Sentences ▶ **327**

Kinds of
Sentences ▶ **327**

Parts of a Sentence

Subject

The **subject** names someone or something. The subject is often doing something.

> The huge balloon is full of water.
>
> (**The huge balloon** is the complete subject.)
>
> My big sister threw the balloon.
>
> (**My big sister** is the complete subject.)
>
> My best friend caught the balloon.
>
> (**My best friend** is the complete subject.)

Simple Subject

The **simple subject** is the main word in the subject.

> The huge balloon is full of water.
>
> (**Balloon** is the simple subject.)
>
> My big sister threw the balloon.
>
> (**Sister** is the simple subject.)
>
> My best friend caught the balloon.
>
> (**Friend** is the simple subject.)

Compound Subject

A **compound subject** is made up of two or more simple subjects joined by *and* or *or.*

> My big sister and my best friend played catch with the balloon.
>
> (**Sister** and **friend** is the compound subject.)

Predicate (verb)

The **predicate** tells what the subject is or does.

> My dog Rocky is the fastest dog on the block.
> (**Is the fastest dog on the block** is the complete predicate.)

> My dog Rocky runs faster than the other dogs.
> (**Runs faster than the other dogs** is the complete predicate.)

Simple Predicate (verb)

The **simple predicate** is the main word in the predicate part of the sentence.

> Rocky is the fastest dog on the block.
> (**Is** is the simple predicate.)

> Rocky runs faster than the other dogs.
> (**Runs** is the simple predicate.)

Compound Predicate (verb)

A **compound predicate** has two or more simple predicates (verbs) joined by *and* or *or.*

> Rocky runs fast and barks loud.
> (**Runs** and **barks** is the compound predicate.)

Types of Sentences

Simple ● A simple sentence has just one thought. It may, however, have two simple subjects or two simple predicates.

> My head hurts. (A basic simple sentence.)

> My head and neck hurt.
> (A simple sentence with two simple subjects.)

> My dog ran and caught the ball.
> (A simple sentence with two simple predicates.)

Compound ● A compound sentence is two sentences joined by a comma and a connecting word (*and, but, or*).

> We went on vacation, and we took our dog.

Kinds of Sentences

Declarative ● A declarative sentence makes a statement.

> The capital of Wisconsin is Madison.

Interrogative ● An interrogative sentence always asks a question.

> Did you know the capital of Nebraska is Lincoln?

Imperative ● An imperative sentence gives a command or makes a request.

> Write the capital of Missouri on the board.

Exclamatory ● An exclamatory sentence shows strong emotion or surprise.

> Cleveland is not the capital of Ohio!

Understanding Our
Language

All the words in our language fit into eight groups.
These word groups are called the **parts of speech**.

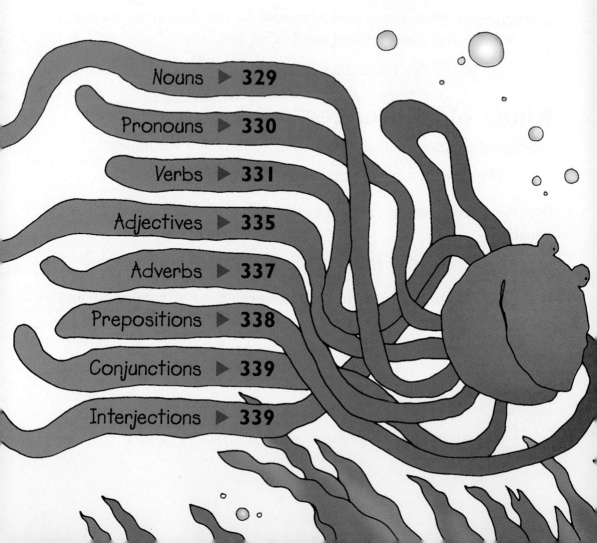

Nouns

A **noun** names a person, a place, a thing, or an idea.

runner   Los Angeles   race   joy

Kinds of Nouns

Common Nouns and Proper Nouns

A **common noun** names any person, place, thing, or idea. A **proper noun** names a specific person, place, thing, or idea.

Common Nouns	Proper Nouns	
girl	Ann	Proper nouns are capitalized.
building	Sears Tower	
team	Atlanta Braves	

Singular and Plural Nouns

A **singular noun** names one person, place, thing, or idea.
A **plural noun** names more than one person, place, thing, or idea.

Singular Nouns	Plural Nouns
kid	kids
bus	buses
can	cans

Possessive Nouns

A **possessive noun** shows ownership.

Our school's colors are blue and white.
(Add 's after a singular noun.)

Both schools' teams played well.
(Add ' after most plural nouns.)

Pronouns

A **pronoun** is a word that takes the place of a noun.

Karl climbed over the fence.
He could have been hurt.
(The pronoun *he* replaces the noun *Karl*.)

The lunchroom was a busy place.
It was very crowded.
(The pronoun *it* replaces the noun *lunchroom*.)

Possessive Pronouns

A **possessive pronoun** shows ownership.

Karl hurt his arm while climbing the fence.
Our lunch table was messy.
Lori left her lunch on their table.

Common Personal Pronouns

Singular Pronouns	Plural Pronouns
I, me, my,	we, us, our,
you, your,	you, your,
he, him, his,	they, them, their
she, her,	
it, its	

Today's
Lunch

- pizza pockets
- carrot sticks
- oatmeal cookies
- milk

Verbs

A **verb** shows action or links two ideas in a sentence.

> The monkey swings through the branches.
> I am happy.

Types of Verbs

Action Verbs

An **action verb** tells what the subject is doing.

> I watched the kangaroo.
> Todd jumped like a kangaroo.

Linking Verbs

A **linking verb** links the subject to a word in the predicate part of a sentence. (The predicate tells what the subject is or does.)

> My teacher is helpful. (The verb links *teacher* to *helpful*.)
> My friends are happy in our school.
> (The verb links *friends* to *happy*.)

Linking Verbs: is, are, was, were, am, be, been

Helping Verbs

A **helping verb** comes before the main verb, and it helps state an action or show time.

> Billie has called two times. (*Has* helps the main verb *called*.)
> Billie will call you again. (*Will* helps the main verb *call*.)

Helping Verbs: has, have, had, will, could, should, would, do, did, may, can

Tense of Verbs

The **tense** of a verb tells when the action takes place. Tense is often shown by endings (play*s*, play*ed*) and by helping verbs (*will* play, *has* played).

Present Tense

Present tense means the action is happening now or that it happens all of the time.

> Jackie plays on our soccer team.
> Our practices help us a lot.

Past Tense

Past tense means the action happened before, or in the past.

> Yesterday Jackie played forward.
> Three girls scored goals.

Future Tense

Future tense means the action will take place at a later time, or in the future.

> Tomorrow Jackie will play goalie.
> We will see a soccer video.

TIP: Some verbs tell the time of the action in other ways.

> Jackie has played soccer for three years.
> Our coach is planning a tournament.
> The soccer field once had been
>   a cow pasture.

Forms of Verbs

Singular and Plural Verbs

The verb in a sentence must agree, or make sense, with the subject. Use a **singular verb** when the subject is singular. Remember that *singular* means "one."

> Kayla eats powdered donuts. (*Eats* is a singular verb.)
>
> She gets powder all over her mouth. (*Gets* is a singular verb.)

Use a **plural verb** when the subject is plural. Remember that *plural* means "more than one."

> The other girls love chocolate donuts. (*Love* is a plural verb.)
>
> They save the frosting part for last. (*Save* is a plural verb.)

Regular Verbs

Many verbs in our language are **regular**. You add *ed* to regular verbs to form the past tense, or when you use a helping verb.

> I play.   Yesterday I played.   I have played.
>
> He kicks.   Yesterday he kicked.   He has kicked.

Irregular Verbs

Some verbs in our language are **irregular**. For most irregular verbs, the word changes when you form the past tense or add a helping verb. (See the next page for a chart.)

> I see.   Yesterday I saw.   I have seen.
>
> She writes.   Yesterday she wrote.   She has written.

TIP: The most common irregular verb is the verb *be*. Different forms of the verb include *am, is, are, was, were,* and *been*.

Common Irregular Verbs

Present	Past	Past with *has, have, had*
am, be	was, were	been
begin	began	begun
break	broke	broken
catch	caught	caught
come	came	come
do	did	done
draw	drew	drawn
drive	drove	driven
eat	ate	eaten
fall	fell	fallen
fly	flew	flown
freeze	froze	frozen
give	gave	given
go	went	gone
grow	grew	grown
hide	hid	hidden, hid
know	knew	known
ride	rode	ridden
ring	rang	rung
run	ran	run
see	saw	seen
sing	sang, sung	sung
speak	spoke	spoken
take	took	taken
throw	threw	thrown
write	wrote	written

Adjectives

An **adjective** is a word that describes a noun or a pronoun.

> Some dogs have funny faces.
> (An adjective usually comes before the word it describes.)

> The fur on a sheepdog is fluffy.
> (Sometimes an adjective comes after a linking verb like *is* or *are*.)

Articles

The articles *a, an,* and *the* are adjectives.

> A pug is a small dog.
> (A is used before words beginning with a consonant sound.)

> The dingo is an Australian dog.
> (*An* is used before words beginning with a vowel sound.)

Kinds of Adjectives

Sensory Adjectives *(what kind)*

Some adjectives describe how a noun looks, sounds, feels, tastes, or smells. These adjectives tell *what kind*.

> Little dogs may have loud barks.

> Our labrador has soft skin.

> Sniffle's treats smell like rotten cheese.

Number Adjectives *(how many)*

Other adjectives describe or tell *how many*.

> Two collies chased our cat.

> Rudy was the first dog in our family.

> I see many dogs every day.

Forms of Adjectives

Describing One Noun (positive form)

An adjective usually describes one person, place, or thing.

> A bloodhound has a wrinkled face.

Comparing Two Nouns (comparative form)

An **adjective** sometimes describes or compares two people, places, or things.

> A bulldog is smaller than a dalmatian.
> (The ending er is added to one-syllable adjectives.)

> A dalmatian is more graceful than a bulldog.
> (*More* is added before many adjectives with two or more syllables.)

Comparing Three or More Nouns (superlative form)

An adjective sometimes describes or compares three or more people, places, or things.

> That Chihuahua is the smallest dog I have ever seen.
> (The ending est is added to one-syllable adjectives.)

> The golden retriever is one of the most beautiful dogs.
> (*Most* is added before many adjectives with two or more syllables.)

Special Forms

The adjectives in this chart use different words to make comparisons.

Positive	Comparative	Superlative
good	better	best
bad	worse	worst
many	more	most

Adverbs

An **adverb** is a word that describes a verb, or tells how an action is done.

> The desert temperature rises quickly.
>
> Desert animals hunt for food nightly.

TIP: Adverbs often end with *ly,* but not always. Words like *not, never, very,* and *always* are common adverbs.

Kinds of Adverbs

Adverbs of Time *(when)*

Some adverbs tell *how often* or *when* an action is done.

> Sand dunes often change their shape.
>
> One group of scientists explored the desert yesterday.

Adverbs of Place *(where)*

Some adverbs tell *where* something happens.

> Another scientist worked nearby.
>
> She stayed outside for a long time.

Adverbs of Manner *(how)*

Adverbs often tell *how* something is done.

> The sun shone brightly.
>
> The horned viper moved silently.

Prepositions

A **preposition** is a word that introduces a prepositional phrase.

> Todd slept under the covers. (*Under* is a preposition.)

> Teddy slept on the chair. (*On* is a preposition.)

Prepositional Phrase

A prepositional phrase begins with a preposition, and it ends with a noun or pronoun.

> Todd has a stuffed animal under his arm.

> Teddy sleeps on his side.

Common Prepositions

about	in	out of	under
above	inside	outside	underneath
across	into	over	until
after	like	past	up
against	near	since	with
along	of	through	within
among	off	to	without
around	on	toward	
at	onto		
before			
behind			
below			
beneath			
between			
by			
during			
for			
from			

Conjunctions

A **conjunction** connects words or groups of words.

> We could use <u>skateboards</u> or <u>rollerblades</u>.
> (*Or* connects two words.)
>
> Maya <u>wrote a poem</u> and <u>sang a song</u>.
> (*And* connects two phrases.)
>
> <u>We ate breakfast early</u>, but <u>we still missed the bus</u>.
> (*But* connects two simple sentences.)

Common Conjunctions

The most common conjunctions are listed here. They are called **coordinate conjunctions**.

> and   but   or   nor   for   so   yet

Other conjunctions help you connect ideas in very specific ways. Here are some of these conjunctions:

> after   before   until   where
> because   since   when   while

> I like to skateboard when it is hot.
> She likes to fish before it rains.

Interjections

An **interjection** is a word or phrase used to express strong emotion or surprise. It is followed by an exclamation point or by a comma.

> Hey! Hold on!
> Wow, look at him go!

5 The Student Almanac

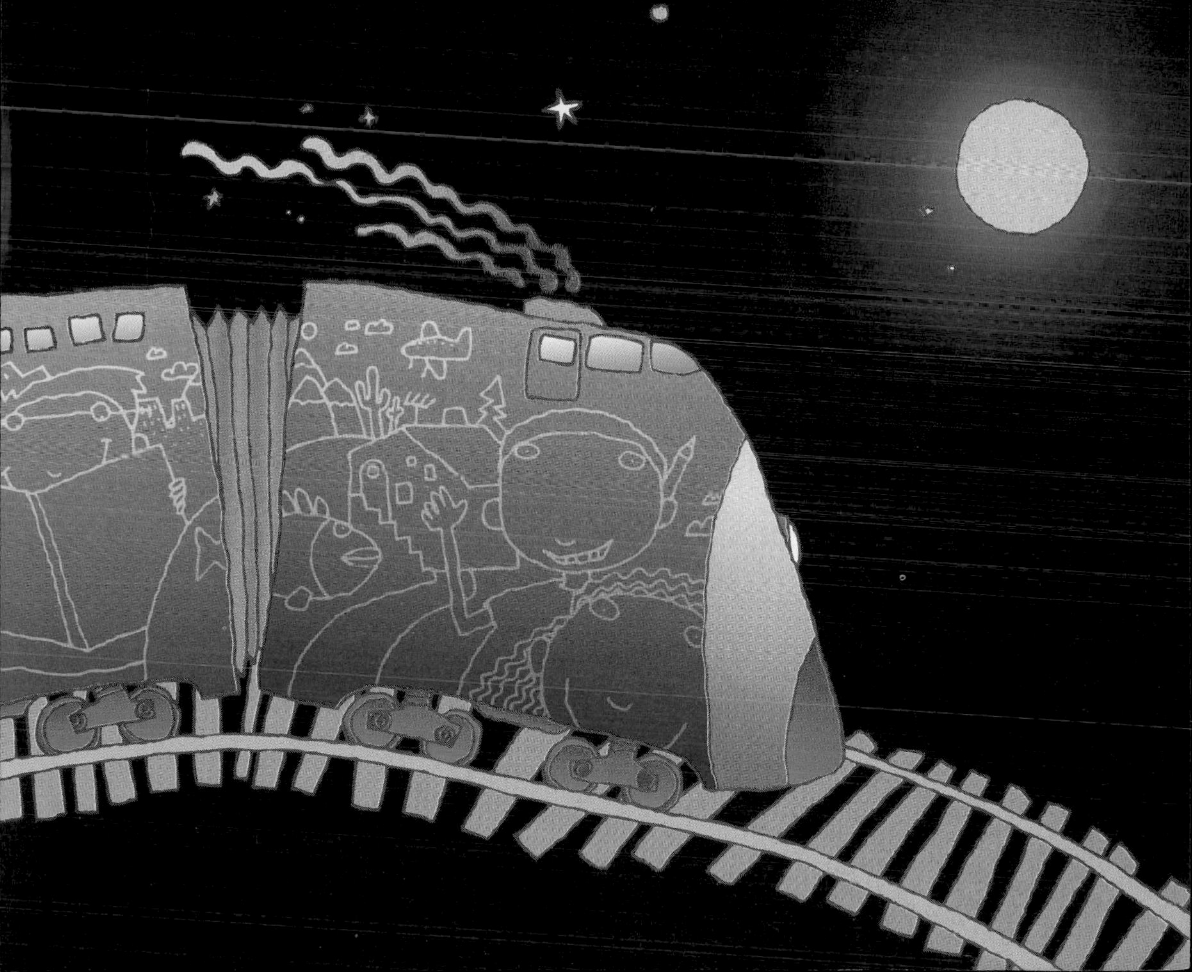

The Student Almanac

Useful Tables and Lists

The tables and lists in this section of your handbook should be both interesting and helpful.

Sign Language

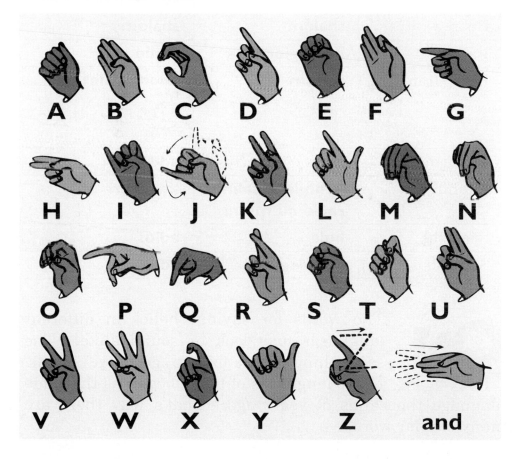

Saying Hello and Good-Bye

There are more than 220 languages in the world today. No wonder people sometimes have trouble speaking to each other, especially when they travel. Here are some "hello" and "good-bye" words that make things a little easier.

Language	Hello or Good Day	Good-Bye
Chinese (Mandarin dialect)	dzău	dzàijyàn
French	bonjour	au revoir
German	Guten Tag	Auf Wiedersehen
Hebrew	shalom	shalom
Italian	buon giorno	addio
Farsi (Iran)	salaam سلام	khoda hafez خدا حافظ
Portuguese	alô	adeus
Swahili	neno la kusalimu rafiki au mtani	kwa heri
Spanish	hola	adiós
Swedish	god dag	adjö

The words for saying "hello" in different languages may look or sound alike. The same thing is true for the "good-bye" words. Many languages of today began as the same language thousands of years ago. That's why there are many similar words.

Animal Facts

Animal	Male	Female	Young	Group	Gestation (days)	Longevity (years)
Bear	He-bear	She-bear	Cub	Sleuth	180-240	18-20 (34)*
Cat	Tom	Queen	Kitten	Clutter/Clowder	52-65	10-17 (30)
Cattle	Bull	Cow	Calf	Drove/Herd	280	9-12 (25)
Chicken	Rooster	Hen	Chick	Brood/Flock	21	7-8 (14)
Deer	Buck	Doe	Fawn	Herd	180-250	10-15 (26)
Dog	Dog	Bitch	Pup	Pack/Kennel	55-70	10-12 (24)
Donkey	Jack	Jenny	Foal	Herd/Pace	340-385	18-20 (63)
Duck	Drake	Duck	Duckling	Brace/Herd	21-35	10 (15)
Elephant	Bull	Cow	Calf	Herd	515-760	30-60 (98)
Fox	Dog	Vixen	Cub/Kit	Skulk	51-60	8-10 (14)
Goat	Billy	Nanny	Kid	Tribe/Herd	135-163	12 (17)
Goose	Gander	Goose	Gosling	Flock/Gaggle	30	25-30
Horse	Stallion	Mare	Filly/Colt	Herd	304-419	20-30 (50+)
Lion	Lion	Lioness	Cub	Pride	105-111	10 (29)
Monkey	Male	Female	Boy/Girl	Band/Troop	149-179	12-15 (29)
Rabbit	Buck	Doe	Bunny	Nest/Warren	27-36	6-8 (15)
Sheep	Ram	Ewe	Lamb	Flock/Drove	121-180	10-15 (16)
Swan	Cob	Pen	Cygnet	Bevy/Flock	30	45-50
Swine	Boar	Sow	Piglet	Litter/Herd	101-130	10 (15)
Tiger	Tiger	Tigress	Cub		105	19
Whale	Bull	Cow	Calf	Gam/Pod/Herd	276-365	37
Wolf	Dog	Bitch	Pup	Pack	63	10-12 (16)

* ( ) Record for oldest animal of this type

MEASUREMENTS

Here are some basic units in the United States system of measurement.

Length (how far)

1 inch (in.) _____ ← ⋯⋯ one inch

1 foot (ft.) = **12 inches**

1 yard (yd.) = **3 feet** = **36 inches**

1 mile (mi.) = **1,760 yards** = **5,280 feet** = **63,360 inches**

Weight (how heavy)

1 ounce (oz.)

1 pound (lb.) = **16 ounces**

1 ton = **2,000 pounds** = **32,000 ounces**

Capacity (how much something can hold)

1 teaspoon (tsp.)

1 tablespoon (tb.) = **3 teaspoons**

1 cup (c.) = **16 tablespoons**

1 pint (pt.) = **2 cups**

1 quart (qt.) = **2 pints** = **4 cups**

1 gallon (gal.) = **4 quarts** = **8 pints** = **16 cups**

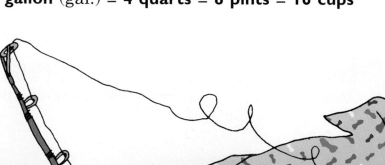

METRIC

Even though the **metric system** is not the official system of measurement in the United States, it is used in science, medicine, and some other areas. This system of measurement is based on units of 10. Here are some common metric measures.

Length (how far)

millimeter

I millimeter (mm) . ◄

I centimeter (cm) = **10 millimeters** _____ ◄····· 10 millimeters

I meter (m) = **100 centimeters** = **1,000 millimeters**

I kilometer (km) = **1,000 meters** = **100,000 centimeters** = **1,000,000 millimeters**

Weight (how heavy)

I gram (g)

I kilogram (kg) = **1,000 grams**

Capacity (how much something can hold)

I milliliter (ml)

I liter (l) = **1,000 milliliters**

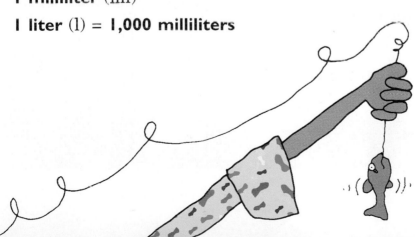

Planet Profiles

Our **solar system** is located in the Milky Way Galaxy. Even though this galaxy has about 100 billion stars, our solar system contains only one star—the sun. The sun is the center of our solar system.

Nine planets and many asteroids, meteors, and comets orbit around the sun. The planets follow regular oval orbits. Mercury, Venus, Mars, and Pluto are similar to Earth in size and chemical makeup. Jupiter, Saturn, Uranus, and Neptune are much larger in size and are surrounded by thick clouds of gas.

	Sun	Moon	Mercury	Venus	Earth
Number of Satellites or Moons	9 planets	0	0	0	1
Diameter	865,400 miles	2,155 miles	3,032 miles	7,519 miles	7,926 miles
Length of One Day*	25 days	27 days	59 days	243 days	24 hours
Length of One Year*		365 days	88 days	225 days	365 days
Average Distance to Sun		93 million miles	36 million miles	67 million miles	93 million miles
Surface Temperature* (Fahrenheit)	11,000° (surface) 27,000,000° (center)	260° (light side) -280° (dark side)	-346° to 950°	850°	-127° to 136°
Weight of a 100-pound person		16	39	90	100

* Approximate numbers

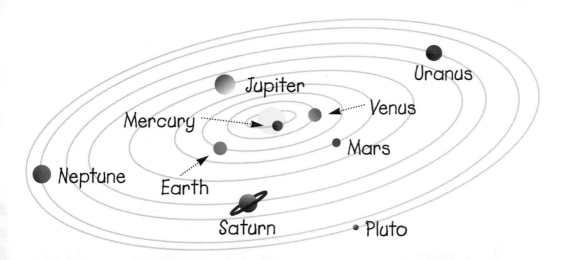

Mars	Jupiter	Saturn	Uranus	Neptune	Pluto
2	16	23	15	8	1
4,194 miles	88,736 miles	74,978 miles	32,193 miles	30,775 miles	1,423 miles
25 hours	10 hours	11 hours	17 hours	16 hours	6 days
687 days	12 years	29 years	84 years	165 years	248 years
142 million miles	484 million miles	887 million miles	1,784 million miles	2,796 million miles	3,666 million miles
-191° to -24°	-236°	-203°	-344°	-360°	-342° to -369°
38	253	107	91	114	1

Using Maps

New countries come into being. Old borders change. It is good to know about these changes. The section that follows will give you the map skills you need to find out about your world.

Reading Maps

There are all kinds of **maps**—weather maps, maps that show the earth's surface, even maps that track hurricanes. Your handbook uses one kind of map, the *political map*. Political maps show how the earth is divided into countries and states. They also show the capitals and major cities.

Map Symbols

Mapmakers use special marks and symbols to show direction (north, east, south, and west). To the right is a *direction finder.* It will show you where north is. If a map does not have a direction finder, north is probably at the top of the page.

The Legend

Important symbols are explained in a box printed on each map. This *legend,* or *key,* helps you understand and use the map. This map legend from the United States map includes symbols for state capitals, cities, and more.

The Map Scale

Legends also have a map scale. The *map scale* shows you how far it is between places. Here is the scale from the map of the United States. It uses inches.

Line up the end of a ruler with the "0" on the scale. How many miles does one inch equal? (Your answer should be 400 miles.) What would two inches equal?

Latitude and Longitude

Latitude ● The lines on a map that go from east to west around the earth are called lines of **latitude**. Latitude is measured in degrees, with the *equator* being 0 degrees (0°). Lines above the equator are called *north latitude*. Lines below the equator are called *south latitude*.

Longitude ● The lines on a map that run from the North Pole to the South Pole are lines of **longitude**. The north-south line measuring 0° passes through Greenwich, England. This line is called the *prime meridian*. Lines east of the prime meridian are called *east longitude*. Lines west of the prime meridian are called *west longitude*.

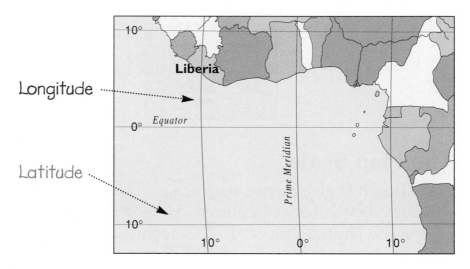

Coordinates ● The latitude and longitude numbers of a country or other place are called its *coordinates*. In each set of coordinates, latitude is written first, then longitude. In the map above, the African country Liberia is located at 7° N, 10° W.

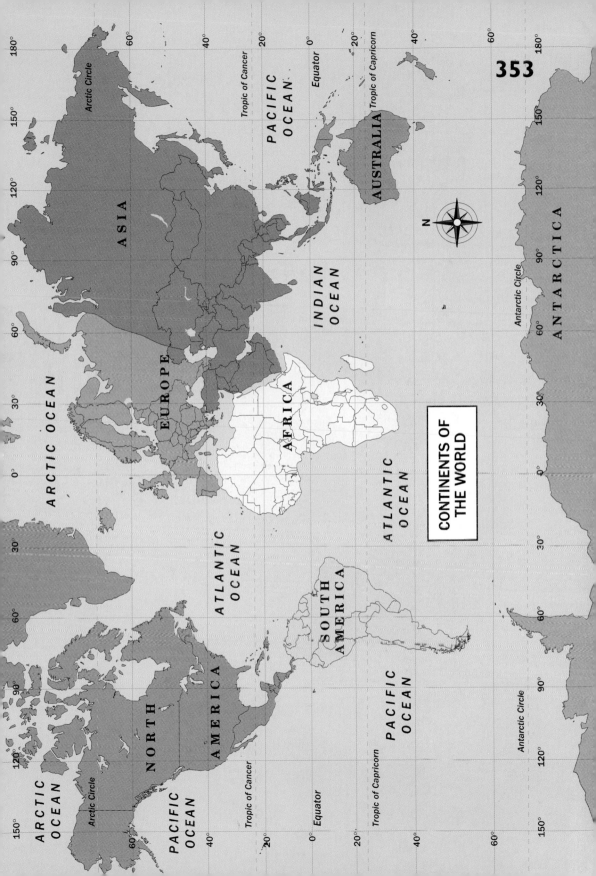

CONTINENTS OF THE WORLD

353

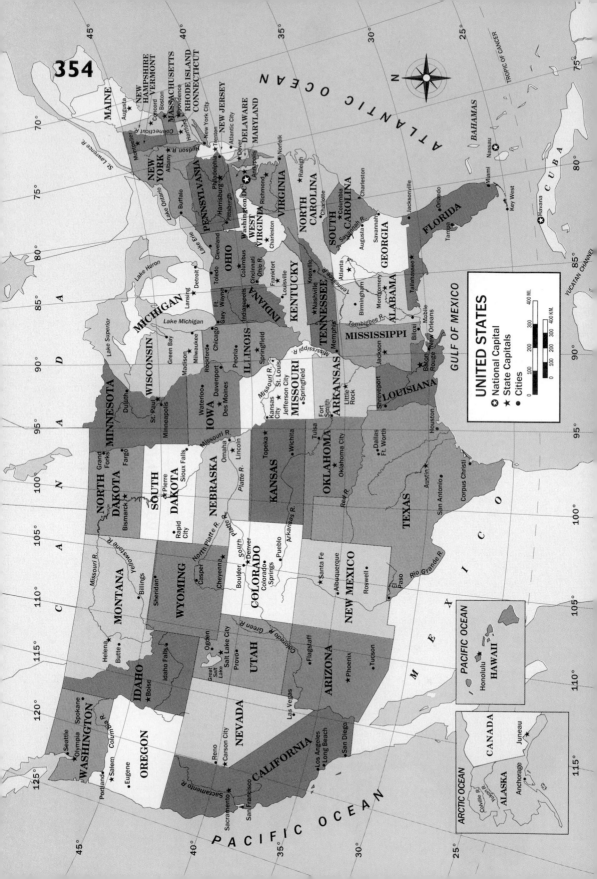

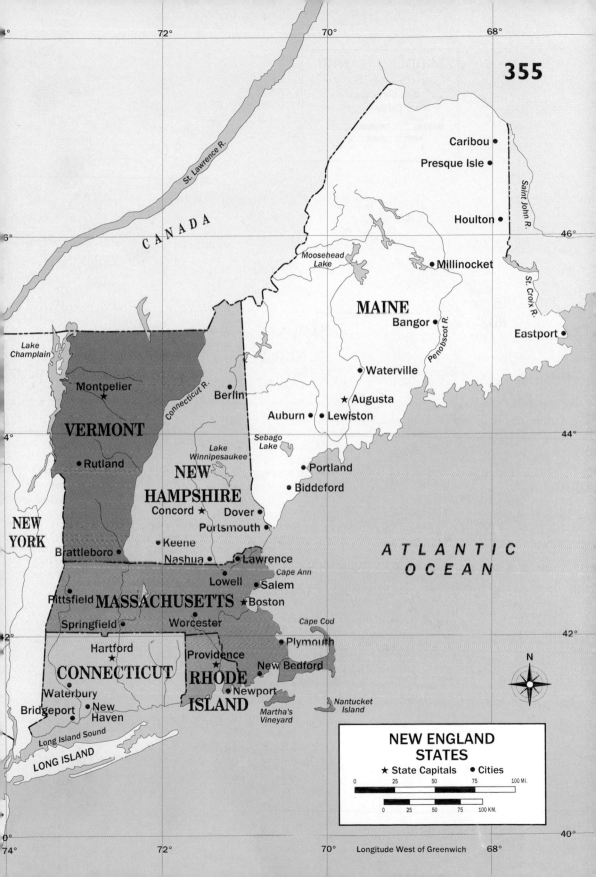

355

CANADA

St. Lawrence R.

Caribou •

Presque Isle •

Houlton •

Saint John R.

Moosehead Lake

Millinocket •

MAINE

Bangor •

Penobscot R.

St. Croix R.

Eastport •

Lake Champlain

Montpelier ★

VERMONT

• Rutland

Connecticut R.

Berlin •

Waterville •

★ Augusta

Auburn • • Lewiston

46°

Lake Winnipesaukee

Sebago Lake

NEW HAMPSHIRE

• Portland

• Biddeford

NEW YORK

Concord ★

Dover •

Portsmouth •

• Keene

Brattleboro •

Nashua • • Lawrence

Lowell •

Cape Ann

• Salem

Pittsfield •

MASSACHUSETTS

★ Boston

Springfield •

Worcester •

Cape Cod

• Plymouth

Hartford ★

Providence •

★

New Bedford •

CONNECTICUT

RHODE ISLAND

• Newport

44°

ATLANTIC OCEAN

42°

N

Waterbury •

Bridgeport •

• New Haven

Martha's Vineyard

Nantucket Island

Long Island Sound

LONG ISLAND

40°

NEW ENGLAND STATES

★ State Capitals   • Cities

0   25   50   75   100 MI.

0   25   50   75   100 KM.

Longitude West of Greenwich

74°   72°   70°   68°

356

MIDDLE ATLANTIC STATES

⊙ National Capital
★ State Capitals ● Cities

0   25   50   75   100 MI.

0   25   50   75   100 KM.

CANADA

Plattsburgh
Lake Champlain

Ogdensburg

Watertown

VERMONT

NEW HAMPSH

Lake Ontario

Lake Oneida

Rome

Rochester
Auburn
Syracuse
Utica
Mohawk R.
Schenectady
Albany ★ Troy

Niagara Falls
Buffalo

NEW YORK

Ithaca
Binghamton

Hudson R.

MASSACHUSETT

Lake Erie

Jamestown
Elmira

Delaware R.

Poughkeepsie

CONNECTICUT

R.I.

Erie

Sharon
New Castle

Allegheny R.

Williamsport
Wilkes-Barre

Scranton

Paterson
Newark

Yonkers
New York

Long Island Sound

Montauk Pt.

OHIO

PENNSYLVANIA

Allentown

Long Island

Pittsburgh
Johnstown

Reading

Trenton

Long Branch

Ohio R.

Harrisburg

Philadelphia

NEW JERSEY

Susquehanna R.

Lancaster

Camden

York

Cumberland

Hagerstown

Wilmington

Atlantic City
Ocean City

Potomac R.

Baltimore

Dover

WEST VIRGINIA

Rockville
Washington

Annapolis

Delaware Bay

Cape May

DISTRICT OF COLUMBIA

DELAWARE

MARYLAND

Salisbury

Chesapeake Bay

VIRGINIA

N

ATLANTIC OCEAN

Cape Charles

NORTH CAROLINA

80° Longitude West of Greenwich 78°

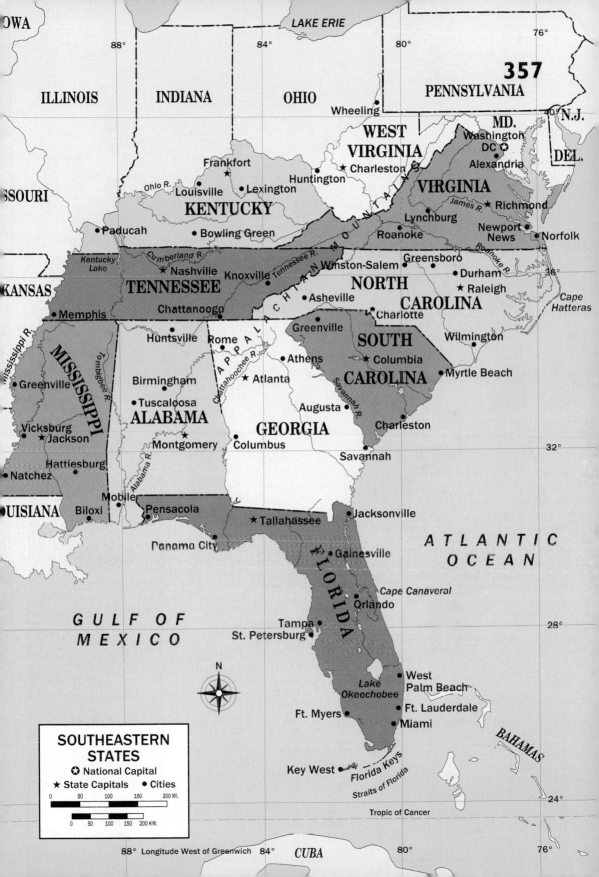

357

SOUTHEASTERN STATES

✪ National Capital
★ State Capitals
• Cities

0 50 100 150 200 MI.

0 50 100 150 200 KM.

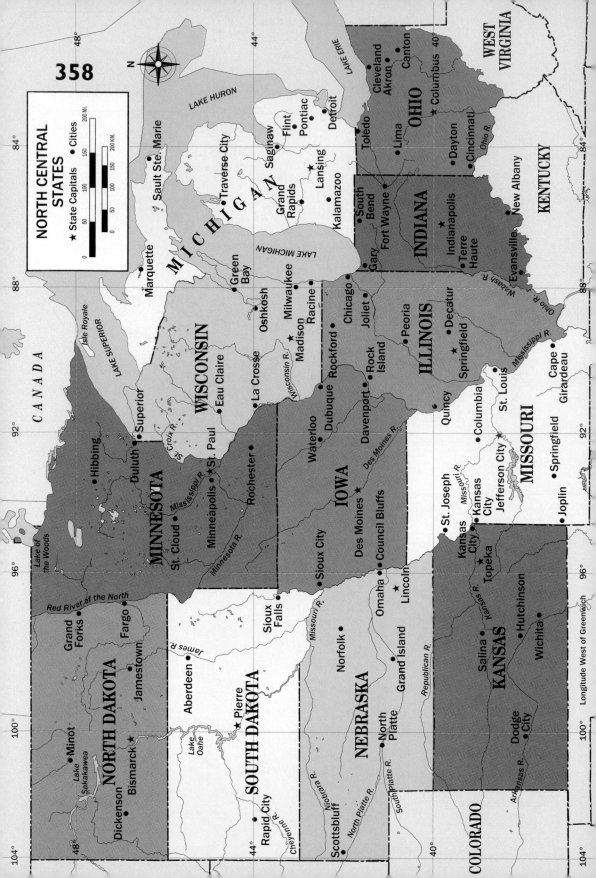

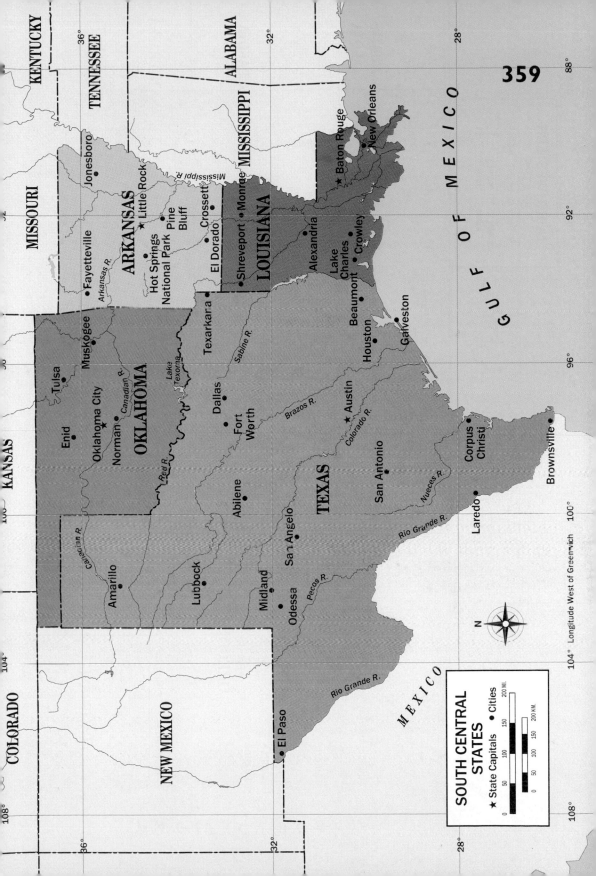

SOUTH CENTRAL STATES

★ State Capitals ● Cities

N

COLORADO

KANSAS

MISSOURI

KENTUCKY

TENNESSEE

ALABAMA

NEW MEXICO

OKLAHOMA

ARKANSAS

MISSISSIPPI

LOUISIANA

TEXAS

MEXICO

GULF OF MEXICO

● Amarillo

Canadian R.

Red R.

● Enid

● Tulsa
● Muskogee
Oklahoma City
● Norman
Lake Texoma
Canadian R.

● Fayetteville
Arkansas R.

● Jonesboro

Mississippi R.

Little Rock ★
● Hot Springs
National Park
● Pine Bluff
● Crossett
● El Dorado

● Monroe
Shreveport ●
Alexandria ●

Baton Rouge ●
★
New Orleans ●

● Texarkana

Sabine R.

Lake Charles ●
● Crowley

● Beaumont

● Houston

Galveston ●

● Dallas
Fort Worth ●

Brazos R.

● Lubbock

● Midland
● Odessa

Pecos R.

● San Angelo

● Abilene

Colorado R.

Austin ★

San Antonio ●

Nueces R.

● Corpus Christi

● Laredo

Rio Grande R.

● Brownsville

● El Paso

Rio Grande R.

104° Longitude West of Greenwich 100°

108°   104°   100°   96°   92°   88°

36°

32°

28°

0   50   100   150   200 MI.

0   50   100   150   200 KM.

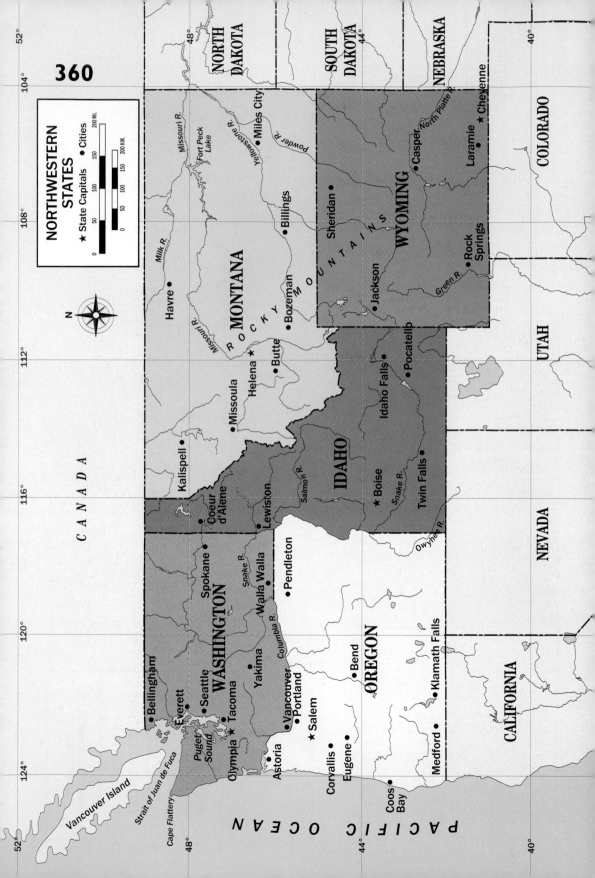

360

NORTHWESTERN STATES

★ State Capitals   • Cities

0   50   100   150   200 MI.

0   50   100   150   200 KM.

CANADA

N

PACIFIC OCEAN

Vancouver Island

Strait of Juan de Fuca

Cape Flattery

Puget Sound

Bellingham •
Everett •
Seattle •
Tacoma •
Olympia ★

WASHINGTON

Spokane •
Yakima •
Walla Walla •
Pendleton •

Snake R.

Columbia R.

Astoria •
Corvallis •
Eugene •
Salem ★
Vancouver •
Portland •
Bend •

OREGON

Coos Bay •
Medford •
Klamath Falls •

Kalispell •
Coeur d'Alene •
Lewiston •

Missoula •
Helena ★
Butte •

MONTANA

Havre •

Milk R.

Missouri R.

Fort Peck Lake

Yellowstone R.

Miles City •

Powder R.

Billings •
Bozeman •

R O C K Y   M O U N T A I N S

IDAHO

Boise ★
Idaho Falls •
Pocatello •
Twin Falls •

Salmon R.

Snake R.

Owyhee R.

Sheridan •

WYOMING

Jackson •

Casper •
Laramie •
Cheyenne ★
Rock Springs •

Green R.

North Platte R.

NORTH DAKOTA

SOUTH DAKOTA

NEBRASKA

COLORADO

UTAH

NEVADA

CALIFORNIA

52°
48°
104°
108°
112°
116°
120°
124°
44°
40°
52°
48°
44°
40°

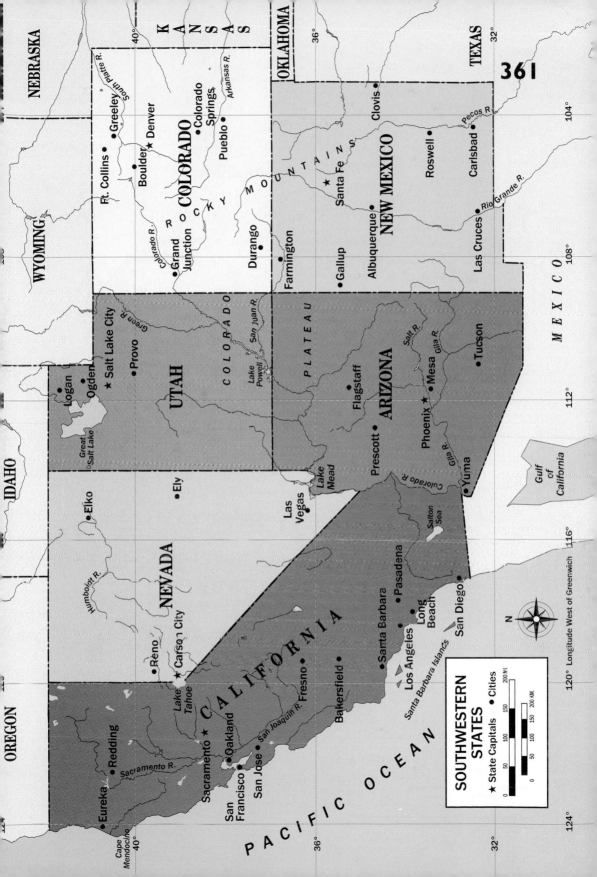

SOUTHWESTERN STATES

★ State Capitals ● Cities

NEBRASKA

KANSAS

OKLAHOMA

TEXAS

WYOMING

IDAHO

OREGON

COLORADO

● Ft. Collins
● Greeley
● Boulder
★ Denver
● Colorado Springs
● Pueblo
● Grand Junction
● Durango

South Platte R.
Arkansas R.
Colorado R.

R O C K Y   M O U N T A I N S

NEW MEXICO

● Clovis
★ Santa Fe
● Roswell
● Carlsbad
● Albuquerque
● Las Cruces
● Gallup
● Farmington

Pecos R.
Rio Grande R.

MEXICO

UTAH

● Logan
● Ogden
★ Salt Lake City
● Provo
● Ely

Great Salt Lake
Green R.
San Juan R.
Lake Powell

C O L O R A D O   P L A T E A U

ARIZONA

● Flagstaff
● Prescott
★ Phoenix
● Mesa
● Tucson
● Yuma

Salt R.
Gila R.
Colorado R.
Lake Mead
Salton Sea

Gulf of California

NEVADA

● Elko
● Reno
★ Carson City
● Las Vegas

Humboldt R.

CALIFORNIA

● Redding
● Eureka
★ Sacramento
● Oakland
● San Francisco
● San Jose
● Fresno
● Bakersfield
● Santa Barbara
● Pasadena
● Los Angeles
● Long Beach
● San Diego

Lake Tahoe
Sacramento R.
San Joaquin R.
Santa Barbara Islands
Cape Mendocino

PACIFIC OCEAN

N

120° Longitude West of Greenwich

0   50   100   150   200 MI.

0   50   100   150   200 KM.

40°
36°
32°
124°
120°
116°
112°
108°
104°

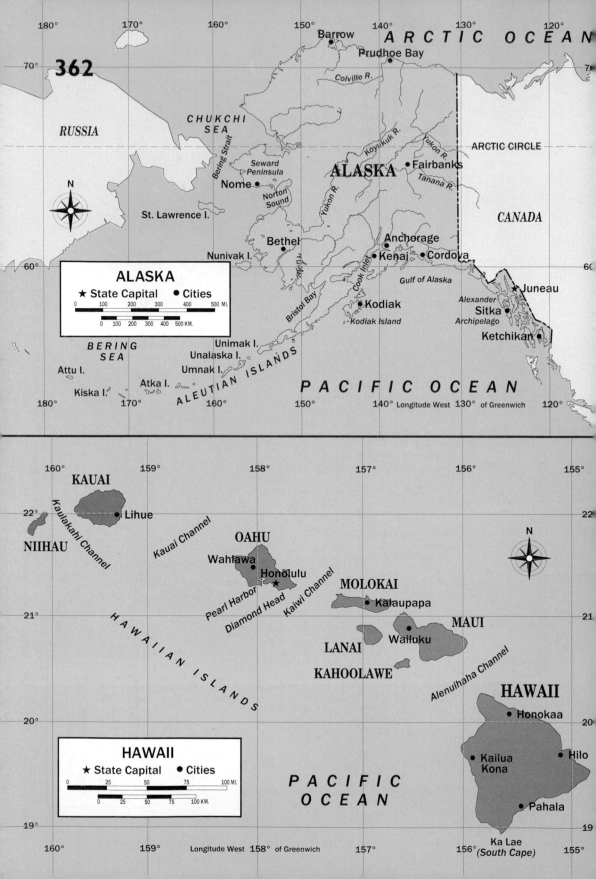

362

ALASKA

ARCTIC OCEAN

Barrow

Prudhoe Bay

Colville R.

CHUKCHI SEA

RUSSIA

ARCTIC CIRCLE

Bering Strait

Koyukuk R.

Yukon R.

Seward Peninsula

Fairbanks

ALASKA

Tanana R.

Nome

Norton Sound

Yukon R.

CANADA

St. Lawrence I.

N

Anchorage

Nunivak I.

Bethel

Kenai · Cordova

Cook Inlet

Gulf of Alaska

Juneau

ALASKA

★ State Capital ● Cities

0   100 200 300 400 500 MI.

0 100 200 300 400 500 KM.

BERING SEA

Kodiak

Kodiak Island

Alexander Archipelago

Sitka

Bristol Bay

Ketchikan

Attu I.

Unimak I.

Unalaska I.

Umnak I.

Atka I.

ALEUTIAN ISLANDS

PACIFIC OCEAN

Kiska I.

Longitude West of Greenwich

160° 159° 158° 157° 156° 155°

KAUAI

Kaulakahi Channel

Lihue

22°

NIIHAU

Kauai Channel

OAHU

Wahiawa

Honolulu

MOLOKAI

Kalaupapa

Pearl Harbor

Diamond Head

Kaiwi Channel

21°

HAWAIIAN ISLANDS

LANAI

Wailuku

MAUI

KAHOOLAWE

Alenuihaha Channel

HAWAII

Honokaa

20°

HAWAII

★ State Capital ● Cities

0   25   50   75   100 MI.

0   25   50   75 100 KM.

PACIFIC OCEAN

Kailua Kona

Hilo

Pahala

19°

Ka Lae (South Cape)

160° 159° Longitude West 158° of Greenwich 157° 156° 155°

Facts About the 50 States

Largest U.S. Cities	Population
New York City, NY	7,322,564
Los Angeles, CA	3,485,398
Chicago, IL	2,783,726
Houston, TX	1,630,553
Philadelphia, PA	1,585,577
San Diego, CA	1,110,549
Detroit, MI	1,027,974
Dallas, TX	1,006,877
Phoenix, AZ	983,403
San Antonio, TX	935,933
San Jose, CA	782,248
Baltimore, MD	736,014
Indianapolis, IN	731,327
San Francisco, CA	723,959
Jacksonville, FL	635,230
Columbus, OH	632,910
Milwaukee, WI	628,088
Memphis, TN	610,337
Washington, DC	606,900
Boston, MA	574,283
Seattle, WA	516,259
El Paso, TX	515,342
Cleveland, OH	505,616
New Orleans, LA	496,938
Nashville-Davidson, TN	488,374

LONGEST RIVERS

	Length (Miles)
Mississippi	2,340
Missouri	2,315
Yukon	1,979
Rio Grande	1,900
Arkansas	1,459
Canadian	1,458
Colorado	1,450
Red	1,290
Columbia	1,243
Snake	1,038

LARGEST LAKES

	Area (Sq. Mi.)
Lake Superior	31,820
Lake Huron	23,010
Lake Michigan	22,400
Lake Erie	9,930
Lake Ontario	7,520
Great Salt Lake (saltwater lake)	1,800

BOUNDARIES BETWEEN

Alaska and Canada
    1,538 miles (2,475 km)
The 48 states and Canada
    3,987 miles (6,416 km)
The 48 states and Mexico
    1,933 miles (3,111 km)

DESERTS

	Area (Sq. Mi.)
Mojave (CA)	15,000
Painted (AZ)	7,000
Great Salt Lake (UT)	4,800
Colorado (CA)	2,500
Black Rock (NV)	1,000

State Capitals and Nicknames

STATE	CAPITAL	STATE NICKNAME
Alabama	Montgomery	*Yellowhammer State*
Alaska	Juneau	*Land of the Midnight Sun*
Arizona	Phoenix	*Grand Canyon State*
Arkansas	Little Rock	*The Natural State*
California	Sacramento	*Golden State*
Colorado	Denver	*Centennial State*
Connecticut	Hartford	*Nutmeg State*
Delaware	Dover	*First State*
Florida	Tallahassee	*Sunshine State*
Georgia	Atlanta	*Peach State*
Hawaii	Honolulu	*Aloha State*
Idaho	Boise	*Gem State*
Illinois	Springfield	*Prairie State*
Indiana	Indianapolis	*Hoosier State*
Iowa	Des Moines	*Hawkeye State*
Kansas	Topeka	*Sunflower State*
Kentucky	Frankfort	*Bluegrass State*
Louisiana	Baton Rouge	*Pelican State*
Maine	Augusta	*Pine Tree State*
Maryland	Annapolis	*Free State*
Massachusetts	Boston	*Bay State*
Michigan	Lansing	*Wolverine State*
Minnesota	St. Paul	*Land of 10,000 Lakes*
Mississippi	Jackson	*Magnolia State*
Missouri	Jefferson City	*Show-Me State*
Montana	Helena	*Treasure State*
Nebraska	Lincoln	*Cornhusker State*
Nevada	Carson City	*Sagebrush State*
New Hampshire	Concord	*Granite State*
New Jersey	Trenton	*Garden State*
New Mexico	Santa Fe	*Land of Enchantment*
New York	Albany	*Empire State*
North Carolina	Raleigh	*Tarheel State*
North Dakota	Bismarck	*Peace Garden State*

STATE	CAPITAL	STATE NICKNAME
Ohio	Columbus	*Buckeye State*
Oklahoma	Oklahoma City	*Sooner State*
Oregon	Salem	*Beaver State*
Pennsylvania	Harrisburg	*Keystone State*
Rhode Island	Providence	*Ocean State*
South Carolina	Columbia	*Palmetto State*
South Dakota	Pierre	*Mount Rushmore State*
Tennessee	Nashville	*Volunteer State*
Texas	Austin	*Lone Star State*
Utah	Salt Lake City	*Beehive State*
Vermont	Montpelier	*Green Mountain State*
Virginia	Richmond	*The Old Dominion*
Washington	Olympia	*Evergreen State*
West Virginia	Charleston	*Mountain State*
Wisconsin	Madison	*Badger State*
Wyoming	Cheyenne	*Equality State*

HIGHEST POINT
Mt. McKinley, AK . . . . 20,320 ft. (6,198 m)

LOWEST POINT
Death Valley, CA . . . . 282 ft. below sea level (86 m)

RAINIEST SPOT
Mt. Waialeale, Kauai, HI . . . . . . 460-inch average annual rainfall

DRIEST SPOT
Death Valley, CA . . . . 1.63-inch average annual rainfall

HIGHEST WATERFALL
Yosemite, CA . . . . .1,430 ft. (436 m)

LARGEST STATE . . . . Alaska 584,412 sq. mi.

SMALLEST STATE . . . . Rhode Island 1,214 sq. mi.

EASTERNMOST POINT . . . . West Quoddy Head, ME

NORTHERNMOST POINT . . . . Point Barrow, AK

SOUTHERNMOST POINT . . . . Ka Lae (South Cape), HI

WESTERNMOST POINT . . . . Cape Wrangell, AK

Improving Math
Skills

When you think of **math**, what do you think of? Adding numbers? Counting change? Measuring with a ruler? Dividing something into equal parts?

Math is this and much more. Learning math is almost like learning a new language. Math has its own special words and symbols. Math also has its own skills and strategies. This chapter will help you understand the language and strategies of mathematics.

What's Ahead

You will learn about a basic process to follow when you work on word problems. You will also learn several problem-solving strategies, including one for solving "brain stretchers." At the end of the chapter, you will find all kinds of helpful charts and tables.

Solving Basic Word Problems

Most of your math assignments include at least two or three **word problems**. And as you know, they can be tricky. The best way to solve word problems is to follow a process. That way you won't miss any important details. Here's a process to try:

Four-Step Process

Read the Problem ● Make sure you understand all of the parts. Look for any key words like "how many" or "in all."

Decide What You Need to Do ● Do you have to add a series of numbers? Do you have to multiply or subtract? Do you have to do more than one thing—maybe add then subtract?

Solve the Problem ● There may be more than one way to solve a problem. Page 369 shows you five strategies for figuring out the same problem. Show all of your work so you can check it later.

Check Your Answer ● Here are two ways to check: (1) You can do the problem again, only in a different way. (2) You can start with your answer and work backward. Let's say, for example, that your answer to a problem is 42. You multiplied 6 times 7 to get that answer. If you divide 42 by 6, you should get 7. Or if you divide 42 by 7, you should get 6.

Sample Word Problem

Read the Problem ● Susan and her best friend, Abbie, are making chocolate cookies for their soccer picnic. They need to know how many cookies to make. There will be 13 people at the picnic, including four parents. They want to give each person three cookies.

Decide What You Need to Do ● After reading the problem, you know that you are looking for a total number of cookies. You also know the basic numbers you have to work with: 13 people with 3 cookies each.

Solve the Problem ● Let's say you decide to **skip-count** by three, 13 times. (See the next page for other strategies.)

3, 6, 9, 12, 15, . . . 39

Check Your Answer ● To check your work, you decide to solve the problem in a different way. You make **tally marks** in 13 groups of three (/// /// /// . . .). You then add up all of your marks. (Your work checks out. The girls need to make 39 cookies.)

Five Problem-Solving Strategies

There are many different ways to solve a word problem. Five different strategies are listed below. (The numbers are from the sample word problem on the last page.)

✱ **Skip-count** by three, 13 times.   3, 6, 9, 12, 15, . . . 39

✱ **Make tally marks.** Put three marks in a group, make 13 groups, and add up all the marks.

/// /// /// /// /// /// /// /// /// /// /// /// ///

✱ **Guess and check.**

Guess: 36 cookies

Check: Divide 36 by 3, 3)‾36. The answer is 12. That's close! Three more cookies are needed, because there are 13 people, not 12. Three more than 36 is 39.

✱ **Use cubes or other counters.** Make 13 groups of 3 counters. Then count them all.

✱ **Write a math problem.** Multiply the number of people by the number of cookies each person would get.

$$
\begin{array}{r}
13 \text{ people} \\
\times\ 3 \text{ cookies (each)} \\
\hline
39 \text{ cookies (total)}
\end{array}
$$

Solving Brain Stretchers

Sometimes you are asked to do problems that can't be solved by simply multiplying or dividing the numbers. We call these types of problems **brain stretchers**. Teachers give you these problems to get you thinking. Here's such a problem:

> You shut your eyes and reach into a jar filled with pennies, nickels, and dimes. You pull out three coins. How much money might be in your hand?

Problem-Solving Strategy

Let's see how one person works on this problem.

✔ **Write equations.** Marissa starts by listing different coin combinations. (Each combination can be called an *equation*.)

> Pennies: 1¢ + 1¢ + 1¢ = 3¢
> Nickels: 5¢ + 5¢ + 5¢ = 15¢
> Pennies and Nickels: 1¢ + 1¢ + 5¢ = 7¢
> 1¢ + 5¢ + 5¢ = 11¢

✔ **Organize a list or table.** Once Marissa has all the penny and nickel combinations, she lists the totals from the smallest number to the largest: 3, 7, 11, 15.

✔ **Look for a pattern.** Marissa notices that each number is four numbers higher than the last.

✔ **Complete the problem.** Marissa completes all of the combinations for the dime. Why don't you complete them along with her to see if the pattern continues.

Symbols, Numbers, and Tables

Use the following pages whenever you need help with your math. The first list includes common math symbols and their meanings. The other tables and charts cover addition, multiplication, rounding numbers, and more.

Math Symbols

+	plus (addition)	°	degree
−	minus (subtraction)	<	is less than
×	multiplied by	>	is greater than
÷	divided by	%	percent
=	is equal to	¢	cents
≠	is not equal to	$	dollars

Addition Facts

Example: Pick a number at the beginning of a row (8). Pick a number at the top of a column (6). Add (8 + 6). Find your answer where the row and column meet (8 + 6 = 14.)

	1	2	3	4	5	(6)	7	8	9	10
1	2	3	4	5	6	7	8	9	10	11
2	3	4	5	6	7	8	9	10	11	12
3	4	5	6	7	8	9	10	11	12	13
4	5	6	7	8	9	10	11	12	13	14
5	6	7	8	9	10	11	12	13	14	15
6	7	8	9	10	11	12	13	14	15	16
7	8	9	10	11	12	13	14	15	16	17
(8)	9	10	11	12	13	(14)	15	16	17	18
9	10	11	12	13	14	15	16	17	18	19
10	11	12	13	14	15	16	17	18	19	20

Multiplication and Division Table

To multiply, do what you did with the "Addition Facts" table (6 x 4 = 24). To divide, do the opposite. Start with a number in the middle (24). Then divide by the number at the top of the column (4), or by the number at the beginning of the row (6). 24 ÷ 4 = 6 or 24 ÷ 6 = 4

X	0	1	2	3	④	5	6	7	8	9	10
0	0	0	0	0	0	0	0	0	0	0	0
1	0	1	2	3	4	5	6	7	8	9	10
2	0	2	4	6	8	10	12	14	16	18	20
3	0	3	6	9	12	15	18	21	24	27	30
4	0	4	8	12	16	20	24	28	32	36	40
5	0	5	10	15	20	25	30	35	40	45	50
⑥	0	6	12	18	㉔	30	36	42	48	54	60
7	0	7	14	21	28	35	42	49	56	63	70
8	0	8	16	24	32	40	48	56	64	72	80
9	0	9	18	27	36	45	54	63	72	81	90
10	0	10	20	30	40	50	60	70	80	90	100

Roman Numerals

I	1	VIII	8	LX	60
II	2	IX	9	LXX	70
III	3	X	10	LXXX	80
IV	4	XX	20	XC	90
V	5	XXX	30	C	100
VI	6	XL	40	D	500
VII	7	L	50	M	1,000

Rounding Numbers

You can round a number to the nearest ten, hundred, thousand, or even million.

Rounding to the Nearest Ten ● If your number
is 32, 32 is closer to 30 than to 40. So, 32 rounded to the nearest ten is 30.

30 31 (**32**) 33 34 35 36 37 38 39 40

The number 36 is closer to 40 than to 30. So, 36 rounded to the nearest ten is 40.

30 31 32 33 34 35 (**36**) 37 38 39 **40**

Numbers ending in 1, 2, 3, or 4 are rounded down. Those ending in 6, 7, 8, or 9 are rounded up. And even though 5 is right in the middle, it is rounded up. So, 35 rounded to the nearest ten is 40.

30 31 32 33 34 (**35**) 36 37 38 39 **40**

Skip-Counting

Count by

2's	2	4	6	8	10	12	14	16	18	20
3's	3	6	9	12	15	18	21	24	27	30
4's	4	8	12	16	20	24	28	32	36	40
5's	5	10	15	20	25	30	35	40	45	50
10's	10	20	30	40	50	60	70	80	90	100

Place Value Chart

7	5	2	,	8	4	3
hundred thousands	ten thousands	thousands	,	hundreds	tens	ones

7 in the hundred thousands' place is	**700,000**
5 in the ten thousands' place is	**50,000**
2 in the thousands' place is	**2,000**
8 in the hundreds' place is	**800**
4 in the tens' place is	**40**
3 in the ones' place is	**3**

You read this six-digit number as **seven hundred fifty-two thousand eight hundred forty-three**.

Fractions

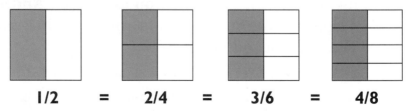

1/2 = 2/4 = 3/6 = 4/8

In 1/2, 1 is the numerator and 2 is the denominator. All the fractions above are called *equivalent fractions*. They all name the same part, or fraction, of the square . . . even though they have different numerators and denominators.

Fractions with the same denominators can easily be compared. (5/8 is greater than 3/8; 1/4 is less than 3/4)

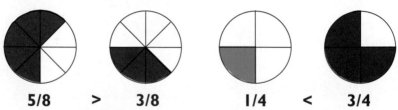

5/8 > 3/8   1/4 < 3/4

Telling Time to the Minute

1:00 ·············▶

When the minute hand (long hand) is on 12, you write 00 for the minutes.

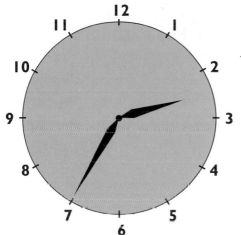

◀·············· # 2:35

When the minute hand is on a number, you can multiply that number by 5. See the multiplication table on page 372 if you have trouble counting by 5's. (5 x 7 = 35)

9:18 ·············▶

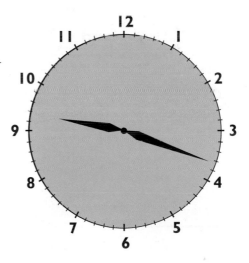

When the minute hand is between numbers, add the number of minute marks past the last number. Remember to first multiply that last number by 5. (3 x 5 = 15; 15 + 3 = 18)

Improving
Handwriting

There are many important parts to writing. You should write about interesting subjects. You should use your best words and sentences. And you should use your best handwriting for your final copies.

This chapter will help you practice your **handwriting**. The pictures below show you how to slant your paper for cursive writing. The next two pages show you how to form manuscript and cursive letters. And the last page offers a handwriting checklist.

Slanting Your Paper

Left Hand   **Right Hand**

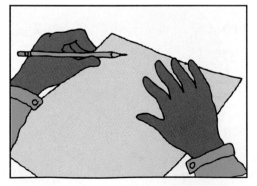

Manuscript Alphabet

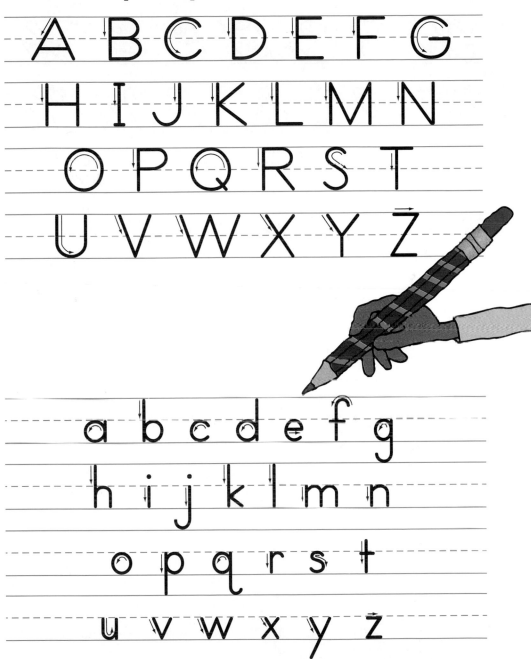

A B C D E F G

H I J K L M N

O P Q R S T

U V W X Y Z

a b c d e f g

h i j k l m n

o p q r s t

u v w x y z

Cursive Alphabet

Handwriting Checklist

☐ Did I sit up straight and slant my paper?

☐ Are all of my letters formed correctly?

☐ Do all of my letters slant the same way?

☐ Are my letters too close or too far apart?

☐ Do I have the right amount of space between each word?

☐ Does my final draft look neat?

☐ Do I like how my final draft looks?

TIP: Save your best handwriting for your final draft.

History
in the Making

The **time line** on the following pages takes you on a trip through time . . . from 1492 when Columbus discovered the West Indies, to 1969 when the first astronauts walked on the moon, to the present time.

Along the way you'll find out some very interesting facts. Do you know when . . .

* forks were first used?
* the first newspaper was printed in the U.S.?
* Washington, D.C., became the capital?
* the first photograph was taken?
* bicycle tires were invented?
* women were given the right to vote?
* CD's were first developed?

Well, you'll find the answers to these and many other questions as you look through the historical time line.

A Closer Look

The historical time line covers the next 10 pages and more than 500 years of history. If you look closely, you'll see that the time line is divided into three parts:

U.S. History ·········▶

Science & Inventions ·········▶

Literature & Life ·········▶

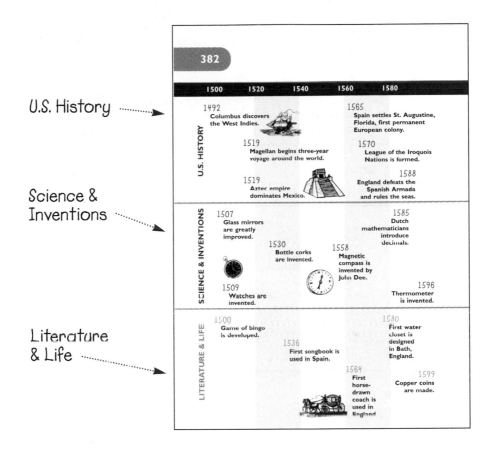

As you use the time line, you can look at each of these three parts to see what was happening in the U.S., science, literature, and everyday life. Looking at history in this way will help you understand what life was really like back then.

We hope you enjoy your travel through time!

1500	1520	1540	1560	1580

U.S. HISTORY

1492
Columbus reaches the West Indies.

1519
Magellan begins three-year voyage around the world.

1519
Aztec empire dominates Mexico.

1565
Spain settles St. Augustine, Florida, first permanent European colony.

1570
League of the Iroquois Nations is formed.

1588
England defeats the Spanish Armada and rules the seas.

SCIENCE & INVENTIONS

1507
Glass mirrors are greatly improved.

1530
Bottle corks are invented.

1509
Watches are invented.

1558
Magnetic compass is invented by John Dee.

1585
Dutch mathematicians introduce decimals.

1596
Thermometer is invented.

LITERATURE & LIFE

1500
Game of bingo is developed.

1536
First songbook is used in Spain.

1564
First horse-drawn coach is used in England.

1580
First water closet is designed in Bath, England.

1599
Copper coins are made.

1600   **1620**   **1640**   **1660**   **1680**   **1700**

1629
Massachusetts Bay
Colony is established.

1607
England
establishes
Jamestown, Virginia.

1673
Marquette and Joliet
explore Mississippi
River for France.

1619
First Africans are brought to Virginia.

1682
William
Penn founds
Pennsylvania.

1620
Plymouth Colony is founded by Pilgrims.

1608
Telescope
is invented.

1643
Evangelista
Torricelli
invents the
barometer.

1671
First calculation
machine is invented.

1629
Human temperature is
measured by a physician
in Italy.

1682
Halley's Comet
is studied by
Edmund
Halley and
named for him.

1609
Galileo makes first observations
with telescope.

1689
Newton describes gravity.

1630
Popcorn is
introduced to
Pilgrims.

1658
First illustrated book for
children, *World of Visible Objects*,
is written by John Comenius.

1653
First
postage
stamps
are used
in Paris.

1685
First
drinking
fountain is
used in
England.

1609
"Three Blind
Mice" is written.

1697
Tales of Mother Goose is
written by Charles Perrault.

1700   **1710**   **1720**   **1730**   **1740**

U.S. HISTORY

1705
Virginia Act establishes public education.

1707
England (English) and Scotland (Scots) become Great Britain (British).

Scotland

England

1718
New Orleans is founded by France.

1733
Molasses Act places taxes on sugar and molasses.

1747
Ohio Company is formed to settle Ohio River Valley.

SCIENCE & INVENTIONS

1709
The pianoforte (first piano) is invented by Christofori Bartolommeo.

1728
First dental drill is used by Pierre Fauchard.

1735
Rubber is found in South America.

1742
Benjamin Franklin invents efficient Franklin stove.

LITERATURE & LIFE

1700
The Selling of Joseph by Samuel Sewall is the first book against slavery of Africans.

1704
First successful newspaper in colonies, *Boston News-Letter*, is published.

1726
Gulliver's Travels is written by Jonathan Swift.

1731
Benjamin Franklin begins the first subscription library.

1744
John Newbery publishes children's book, *A Little Pretty Pocket-Book*.

| 1750 | 1760 | 1770 | 1780 | 1790 | 1800 |

1750
Flatbed boats and Conestoga wagons begin moving settlers west.

1765
Stamp Act tax is imposed on colonies by Britain.

1776
Declaration of Independence is signed on July 4.

1775
First battles of the Revolutionary War are fought.

1787
The United States Constitution is signed.

1781
British surrender October 19.

1789
George Washington is elected president.

1752
Benjamin Franklin discovers lightning is a form of electricity.

1764
"Spinning Jenny" for cotton is invented.

1770
First steam carriage is invented.

1783
First balloon is flown.

1793
Eli Whitney invents the cotton gin to take seeds out of cotton.

1798
Eli Whitney invents mass production.

1752
First general hospital is established in Philadelphia.

1765
First novel written for children is *Little Goody Two-Shoes*.

1786
First ice-cream company in America begins production.

1782
The American bald eagle is first used as a symbol of the United States.

1757
Streetlights are installed in Philadelphia.

1769
Venetian blinds are first used.

1795
Food canning is introduced.

1800	1810	1820	1830	1840

U.S. HISTORY

1800
Washington, D.C., becomes U.S. capital.

1804
Lewis & Clark explore Louisiana and Northwest territories.

1819
U.S. acquires Florida from Spain.

1836
Texans defend Alamo.

1838
Cherokee Nation forced west on "Trail of Tears."

1848
Gold is found in California.

1830
Native Americans are forced west by the Indian Removal Act.

SCIENCE & INVENTIONS

1800
The battery is invented by Count Volta.

1802
Steamboat is built by Robert Fulton.

1816
Stethoscope is invented.

1836
Samuel Morse invents telegraph.

1846
Elias Howe invents sewing machine.

1839
Bicycle is invented by Kirkpatrick Macmillan.

LITERATURE & LIFE

1814
Francis Scott Key writes "The Star-Spangled Banner."

1816
Niepce takes first photograph.

1804
First book of children's poems is published.

1823
A Visit from St. Nicholas is written by Clement Clark Moore.

1834
Louis Braille perfects a letter system for the blind.

1835
Hans Christian Andersen publishes *Tales Told to Children*.

1849
Safety pin is invented.

| 1850 | 1860 | 1870 | 1880 | 1890 | 1900 |

1860
Abraham Lincoln is
elected 16th president.

1861
Civil War begins.

1865
Civil War ends.

1862
Lincoln proclaims abolition of slavery.

1869
Coast-to-coast railroad is finished in Utah.

1876
U.S. Centennial
is celebrated.

1898
U.S. defeats
Spain in
Spanish-
American
War.

1851
Isaac Singer
produces a
sewing machine.

1860
Internal
combustion
engine is
built.

1876
Alexander
Graham Bell
invents
telephone.

1879
Edison
invents the
lightbulb.

1893
Charles and
Frank
Duryea
build first
successful
U.S.
gasoline
automobile.

1896
Marconi invents
wireless radio.

1865
*Alice's
Adventures in
Wonderland* is
written.

1876
National
Baseball
League is
established.

1866
Root beer is introduced
by Elmer Hires.

1892
"Pledge of
Allegiance"
is written by
F. Bellamy.

1888
Bicycle tires
are introduced
by John Dunlop.

1900	1905	1910	1915	1920

U.S. HISTORY

1903
Orville and Wilbur Wright fly first successful airplane.

1909
National Association for the Advancement of Colored People (NAACP) is founded.

1917
United States enters World War I.

1918
World War I ends in Europe.

1914
Panama Canal opens.

1920
Women are given right to vote.

SCIENCE & INVENTIONS

1901
Walter Reed discovers yellow fever comes from mosquitos.

1904
New York City develops subway system.

1913
Henry Ford establishes assembly line for automobiles.

1915
Coast-to-coast telephone system is established.

1921
Vaccine for tuberculosis is discovered.

1922
Electron scanner for television is developed.

LITERATURE & LIFE

1900
Hot dog is created in New York City.

1900
The Wonderful Wizard of Oz is written by L. Frank Baum.

1903
First World Series is played.

1917
American Girl magazine is published by Girl Scouts.

1913
Boy's Life magazine is published by Boy Scouts.

1920
First radio station, KDKA, is founded in Pittsburgh.

| 1925 | 1930 | 1935 | 1940 | 1945 | 1950 |

1927
Charles Lindbergh flies solo across the Atlantic Ocean.

1941
U.S. enters World War II Dec. 7.

1945
World War II ends.

1945
United States joins the United Nations.

1933
President Franklin Roosevelt begins New Deal to end Great Depression.

1947
Jackie Robinson becomes first black major league baseball player.

1926
Alexander Fleming develops penicillin.

1938
Modern-type ballpoint pens are developed.

1931
Empire State Building (102 stories, 1,250 feet) is completed as tallest in the world.

1938
First photocopy machine is produced.

1935
Radar is invented.

1940
Enrico Fermi develops nuclear reactor.

1925
Potato chips are produced in New York City.

1931
"Star-Spangled Banner" becomes U.S. national anthem.

1937
Snow White and the Seven Dwarfs movie is made.

1946
Highlights for Children magazine is published.

1928
My Weekly Reader magazine is founded.

1938
Superman "Action Comics" are created.

1950	1955	1960	1965	1970

U.S. HISTORY

1950
United States enters Korean War.

1954
Korean War ends.

1959
Alaska and Hawaii become states.

1961
Alan Shepard is first U.S. astronaut in space.

1963
President John F. Kennedy is assassinated.

1965
U.S. troops are sent to Vietnam.

1968
Martin Luther King, Jr., is assassinated.

1969
Neil Armstrong and Buzz Aldrin are first men on moon.

SCIENCE & INVENTIONS

1951
Fluoridated water is discovered to prevent tooth decay.

1957
Russia launches first satellite, *Sputnik I.*

1958
Stereo long-playing records are produced.

1963
Cassette music tapes are developed.

1971
Space probe *Mariner* maps surface of Mars.

1974
Sears Tower (110 stories, 1,454 feet) is built in Chicago.

LITERATURE & LIFE

1950
Peanuts comic strip is created by Charles Schulz.

1951
Fifteen million American homes have television.

1955
Cat in the Hat is written by Theodor "Dr. Seuss" Geisel.

1957
Elvis Presley is the most popular rock 'n' roll musician in U.S.

1964
The Beatles appear on *The Ed Sullivan Show.*

1969
Sesame Street television show begins.

1975	1980	1985	1990	1995	2000

1981
Sandra Day
O'Connor becomes
first woman on
Supreme Court.

1989
Berlin Wall
in Germany
is torn
down.

1994
Earthquake rocks
Los Angeles.

1975
Vietnam
War
ends.

1995
Federal
building
bombed in
Oklahoma
City.

1983
Sally Ride
becomes first
U.S. woman
in space.

1991
Persian Gulf War
"Operation Desert
Storm" begins.

1976
Concorde
becomes
world's first
supersonic
passenger
jet.

1983
Pioneer 10 space
probe passes
Neptune and
leaves solar
system.

1991
Scientists report
growing danger of hole
in Earth's ozone layer.

1993
Apple's Newton
Writing-Pad
computer is
produced.

1984
Compact discs (CD's)
are developed.

1976
United States
celebrates
Bicentennial.

1986
Martin Luther
King Day is
proclaimed a
national holiday.

1993
Jurassic Park features
new computer film-
making techniques.

1977
Star Wars
becomes
largest money-
making movie
of all time.

1987
The Whipping Boy wins
Newbery Award.

1988
Thirty million U.S. schoolchildren
have access to computers.

Index

The **index** helps you find information in your handbook. Let's say you want to learn how to write a haiku poem. You can look in your index under "haiku" or under "poetry" for help. (See if you can find the correct pages for haiku poetry in the index.)

Question, 303, 327
Question mark, 303, 327
Quotation marks,
    Punctuating spoken words, 302
    Punctuating titles, 302

Rambling sentence, 71
Reading,
    Graphics, 193-197
    Mapping, 204-205
    Prefix, suffix, root, 199, 214-223
    Reviewing, 201
    Strategies, 198-199, 200-205
    Vocabulary, 207-213
Reading journal, 79
Realistic stories, writing, 159-163
    Model, 160
Red/read, 321
Reference books, 142-143
Repeating sounds, 183
Report, classroom, 144-151
    Gathering grid, 148
    Model, 145
Response sheets, writing, 51
Retelling, 205
Review, book, 116-121
    Models, 117, 120
Revising, 15, 18, 43-47, 50
    Checklist, 47
Rhyme, 183, 185
Right/write, 321
Road/rode/rowed, 321
Roman numerals, 372
Roots, 214, list of, 219-223
Run-on sentence, 71

Salutation, 92-93, 124-125
Schedules, 197
Scheduling work, 277-279
Scoring a poem, 243
Scripting a poem, 242
Sea/see, 322
Seen/scene, 322
Selecting subjects, 35-37
Sensory detail, 46
Sent/scent/cent, 319
Sentence, 69-71, 324-327
    Combining, 72-73
    Completion, 70
    Fragment, 71
    Kinds of, 327
    Parts of, 70, 325-326
    Problems, 71
    Rambling, 71
    Run-on, 71
    Types of, 327
Series, words in a, 73, 297
Setting, 121
Setting goals, 277-279
Sew/so/sow, 322
Sharing in groups, 280-283
Short-answer test, 290
Short talk, giving, 246-251
    Note cards, 249
Show don't tell, 46
Sign language, 343
Signature, letter, 92-93, 124-125
Signs, and symbols, 194
Simile, 183
Simple,
    Predicate (verb), 326
    Sentence, 327
    Subject, 325
Skills,
    Listening, 49, 238-239, 280-283
    Test-taking, 284-291
    Thinking, 263-275
    Viewing, 233-237